Revolt
from the
Heartland

The Struggle for
an Authentic
Conservatism

Revolt
from the
Heartland

Joseph Scotchie

Transaction Publishers
New Brunswick (U.S.A.) and London (U.K.)

Library of Congress Catalog Number: 2002075516
ISBN: 0-7658-0128-0
Printed in the United States of America

Library of Congress Cataloging-in-Publication Data

Scotchie, Joseph, 1956-
    Revolt from the heartland : the struggle for an authentic conservatism / Joseph Scotchie.
        p. cm.
    Includes bibliographical references (p.) and index.
    ISBN 0-7658-0128-0 (alk. paper)
    1. United States—Politics and government—1989- 2. United States—Politics and government—Philosophy. 3. Conservatism—United States. 4. Right and left (Political science) 5. Populism—United States. 6. Globalization—Political aspects—United States. 7. Anti-imperialist movements—United States. I. Title.

E839.5 .S38 2002
320.52'0973—dc21   2002075516

Contents

Introduction

Referring to Pat Buchanan's call to "save the old Republic" with an America First foreign and domestic agenda, Bill Kauffman joked that "[while] this salvage job may make raising The Titanic seem like plucking a toy boat from a bathtub, what patriot cannot heed the call?" [1]

This underfunded, mostly unknown movement (referred to in this volume as both paleoconservative and Old Right) provided the intellectual firepower behind the troubled populism of the 1990s. In that decade, the Old Right and its grass-roots allies made plenty of noise: the renegade candidacies of Buchanan and Ross Perot, a spirited opposition to global free trade deals and various American wars around the world, support for initiatives in California opposing illegal immigration and affirmative action, plus support also for term limits. These are just some of the issues where such populists took on a well-funded left-right establishment. The revolt against globalism has, at the least, roiled American presidential politics. Perot's candidacies took huge chunks out of the Republican Party's old Nixon-Reagan coalition, making life especially miserable for George Bush's 1992 re-election bid. In 2000, Ralph Nader's left-leaning populism did not do as well as Perot's previous campaigns, but his vote total was enough to deny Al Gore the presidency.

In all, it's been too much noise for the conservative establishment to take. Conservatives claim opposition to ethnic cleansing in Yugoslavia, but at home, they have taken part in some ideological cleansing of their own. Nearly all of the living writers mentioned in this volume have seen their careers targeted simply for taking contrary positions on a globalist agenda where both the Beltway Right and the Clinton administration found common agreement. Joe Sobran's antiwar stance during the Persian Gulf War eventually led to his firing from his senior editor position at *National Review*. A few years earlier, that publication's senior book editor, Chilton Williamson, Jr., left *NR* after failing to convince his colleagues to agree with his own restrictionist views on immigration. On it went. In 1995, Samuel Francis was fired from the *Washington Times* after nine years of service to that publication—this despite the fact that Francis had won the only two Distinguished Writing Awards of the American Society of Newspaper Editors in the *Times'* brief history. Paul Gottfried lost a teaching position at American University in Washington after a cabal of East Coast conservatives voiced their objection to such a hiring. Pat Buchanan retained both his nationally syndicated column and his chair on the popular cable talk show, *Crossfire*, but his presidential campaigns were sent reeling by a string of unprecedented smear campaigns, orchestrated by all elements of the American media.[2]

The lack of access to the mass media is not all that hampers the Old Right. It also has suffered from a lack of funds, namely in the form of grants from the right's famed "four sisters" (Olin, Bradley, Scaife, and Smith-Richardson foundations). While the Rockford Institute, the nerve center of paleoconservative thought, has a budget of a little over $1 million, the Heritage Foundation and the American Enterprise Institute, both located in Washington, have budgets of over $35 million per annum.

Still, the new Old Right has articulated an arresting worldview, presented by an array of learned and provocative writers: Francis, Sobran, Buchanan, Gottfried, Williamson, plus Thomas Fleming, Clyde Wilson, Lew Rockwell, and Bill Kauffman, among others. This volume examines the intellectual forerunners to today's Old Right: the anti-Federalists who opposed ratification of the U.S. Constitution; opponents of empire who stood against the Spanish-American War, Woodrow Wilson's League of Nations, and Franklin Roosevelt's New Deal; plus those, past and present, who have cast a cold eye on the legacy of the War Between the States. The importance of the classics, the benefits of republican living, a recognition of regional cultures, the primacy of the family over the state, a moral case against immigration, a practical case against an interventionist foreign policy, and in general, a Tenth Amendment approach to issues ranging from education to such recurring ones as school prayer and abortion are other characteristics that distinguish the Old Right. Paleoconservatives have something to say, but whether people care to listen is another subject they do not shy away from addressing, either.

1

Reading America

"Our enemies realize that to control the past is to enjoin the future." So claimed M.E. Bradford in 1986, during a time of Old Right discontent with the administration of Ronald Reagan. When Bradford spoke of "our enemies," he meant not only the left, but also elements of American conservatism then at loggerheads with the Old Right. Liberals are smart enough to know that the culture wars represent the most important political battles. Paleoconservatives share that sentiment, too. Throughout the twentieth century, American conservative intellectuals have long considered themselves an embattled minority, out of step with an ever-daunting "age of enormity." The result has been an intense study not only of America's wrong turns, but Western civilization's as well.[1]

Richard Weaver, for instance, lamented the collapse of the High Middle Ages, the era of knighthood and chivalry. Followers of Edmund Burke, especially Russell Kirk, point to the French Revolution and the rise of egalitarianism under the bloodied slogan of "liberty, equality, fraternity" as paving the way for twentieth-century-style tyranny. Eric Voeglin, the famed emigré political scientist, singled out the gnosticism of the first and second centuries, where the first major revolt against Christian dogma took place. What such theses have in common is the leveling of a responsible hierarchy in favor of a revolution characterized by state planning and social engineering. Man may think he is his own "priest and ethics professor," when in fact, he is a willing ward of the state. Furthermore, most of these calamities point to the fall of a non-materialistic, generally religious society.

Such upheavals, with the exception of the French Revolution, took place by the time the American Revolutionary War was won, the U.S. Constitution was ratified, and with it, the birth of the first republic in

1

the modern world. For the Old Right, this modest attempt at self-government represented at least a chance to build a "refuge from the historical process," a Switzerland in North America that might escape the decadence and torpor nations inevitably fall into. The struggle to maintain a republic has been the great drama of American history.[2]

The debate over the ratification of the Constitution itself represented a high-water mark in the intellectual life of the United States. Thirteen colonies had fought a long, eight-year struggle to free themselves from the most powerful nation on earth; a nation to which the leaders of the revolution had once willingly pledged their allegiance. This new-found freedom could easily be squandered by creating a government with the same tyrannical impulses. The ratification debate was highly philosophical, graced with the Founders' immense knowledge of world history. It focused also on the nature of man and what form of government might best serve to curb his evil instincts. But even that document, widely hailed as America's great gift to the world, has been a cause of great scrutiny, if not real misgivings among Old Right scholars.

Even more so than Russell Kirk or Murray Rothbard, Bradford, a longtime professor of English at the University of Dallas before his death in 1993, exerted the greatest intellectual influence on the post-Cold War Old Right. For example, the back cover of his 1991 collection, *The Reactionary Imperative*, contains praise from a Who's Who of important paleoconservatives: Kirk, Fleming, Clyde Wilson, Samuel Francis, U.S. Senator John East, Chilton Williamson, Jr., and Tom Landess. For Bradford, the convention in Philadelphia represented a great showdown on the desirability of a national government between the Federalists and anti-Federalists. Bradford's two great heroes of the founding era were Virginia's Patrick Henry and John Dickinson of Pennsylvania. Henry opposed ratification of the Constitution, while Dickinson, an opponent of the Declaration of Independence, went along with James Madison's final document.

An all-but-forgotten figure today, Dickinson accepted, but did not vote for the Declaration of Independence, disliking Thomas Jefferson's "vehement language" concerning what forever could be interpreted as an endorsement for a disastrous equality of results. Dickinson's writings, especially his "Letters From A Pennsylvania Farmer," were extremely popular in their day, giving great clarity to the colonies' revolutionary fervor. His only rival in this sphere was the British author, Tom Paine. But Dickinson stood on much firmer ground than the mercurial Paine. He counseled that history, with its never-ending story of man's triumphs and follies, and not reason, should be the young republic's guide when drafting a constitution. Dickinson understood that American-style liberty was rooted firmly in the "English political identity," itself unique in its emphasis on private property and equality under the law.[3]

For Bradford, Patrick Henry was the age's greatest prophet of political decentralization. An opponent of ratification, Henry strongly advised his fellow Southerners not to make a political alliance with gnostic New Englanders. Patrick Henry was the true spokesman of the American Revolution, the electrifying orator who energized the resistance to the Stamp Act and other regressions by King George III. Henry viewed the Revolutionary War as a matter of self-defense and self-preservation; simply the right of the colonies to have self-government. As Russell Kirk long noted, the war did not represent a "revolution made" but one prevented. The real revolutionary was King George III and his attempts to deny the colonies liberties they had long enjoyed under English law.

Henry, however, feared the Federalists' constitution would upend the gains of the war. Their document would lead to the "divinization of the state" with "men living for government" and government itself "existing for the sake of ideology alone." A "remote, arbitrary, potentially unfriendly" government might take hold. Patrick Henry's America, Bradford observed, did not "exist to pursue certain military, economic, moral or philosophical objectives." Rather, it was comprised of people "living privately in communities, within the ambit of family and friends; living under the eye of God out of the memory of their kind." While Dickinson recoiled at the "horror of a government forever performing experiments," Henry held the same feelings for a "totally politicized world."[4]

An unabashed admirer of these two giants, Bradford's sympathies were with Henry and the anti-Federalists. Following the Revolutionary War, the Articles of Confederation, whose first draft was penned by the ubiquitous Dickinson, allowed for an alliance between the thirteen states. Each of the former colonies remained a sovereign political entity. Recalling the Old Right debates of the 1930s, Murray Rothbard noted that some conservatives had wanted to "go to all the way back to the Articles of Confederation." In that same spirit, Lew Rockwell could speak of our "badly flawed Constitution," while Clyde Wilson would lament that document's call for "the general welfare" to be tended to, undoubtedly because such a sentiment has forever been interpreted as an excuse for extensive, never-ending government action.[5]

A strict reading of the Constitution, one free of incorporation clauses and hidden meanings, is good enough for the Old Right. Still, it is easy to see why they have always felt a kinship with the anti-Federalists. Not only did they fervently oppose centralized power; the anti-Federalists also placed a great emphasis on a generally homogeneous, religious, and moral society. As with their leader, Patrick Henry, the opposition party feared a strong national government that would eventually undermine the sovereignty of the states. They worried that the Federalists, with such a government, would then lead the young nation on the road toward empire. The anti-Federalists were not, of course, against individual freedom, but such freedom could only endure if it were complemented by republican virtues, by a people with a strong interest in all political affairs, local, national, and foreign, a people whose "manners, sentiments, and interests" were similar. The naturalization of aliens, for instance, should be the domain not of the federal government, but of the states. Why? Because, the states represented a government close to home, they were sensitive to the integrity of local cultures. Here, the anti-Federalists were influenced by the example of Pennsylvania, where not only Benjamin Franklin worried that excessive German immigration might destroy the Anglo-Saxon-Celtic character of that commonwealth.[6]

Furthermore, the anti-Federalists did not view wealth as the measure of a man—or of a nation. Preferring a "simple [and] sturdy" people, the anti-Federalists also believed that a wholly materialistic populace would inevitably become soft, decadent, and spoiled, incapable (and undeserving) of self-government. A strong Christian morality was the underpinning of a virtuous society. The anti-Federalists, according to Herbert Storing, would have strengthened the religious establishments that already existed in several of the former colonies. "Without the prevalence of Christian piety and morals," one Charles Turner claimed, "the best republican Constitution can never save us from slavery and ruin."[7]

The great debate was an early example of the losing side exerting influence over the final outcome. While the Federalists secured ratification, the anti-Federalists won the intellectual contest, namely, the war against centralized power. "[Their] ideas," Samuel Francis maintains, "...have informed the long American tradition of resistance to the leviathan state...appearing in the thought and on the lips of John Randolph, John C. Calhoun, the leaders of the Confederacy, the Populists of the late nineteenth century and the Southern Agrarians of the early twentieth."[8]

Opponents of empire, most paleos, nonetheless, have said little about the War of 1812, the Indian wars throughout the continent, or the Mexican War, and the idea of Manifest Destiny itself. Once Thomas Jefferson brilliantly executed the Louisiana Purchase from a retreating French Empire, America's expansion to the Pacific Coast was inevitable. Nineteenth-century America was a young nation with high birthrates, an expanding economy, one populated by a confident, industrious, and often highly moralistic people. Its historic victory over Great Britain only seemed to make the nation more eager to take on all comers. Americans perceived that good land in Texas and the Southwest was being squandered by the Mexican government. That same government also welcomed Anglo settlers into Texas. Some members of the Mexican parliament warned about these Anglos and their desire for land. However, such warnings went unheeded until the newcomers began to outnumber the Mexicans in Texas, a demographic revolution that led to Texas's independence and its eventual inclusion into the United States. Immigration transformed Texas from a Mexican entity to an American one.[9]

America's early wars and land expansions, as Pat Buchanan has contended, were a combination of defensive actions and the result of European powers leaving North America. A declining Spanish Empire put Florida up for grabs. American control brought order to that strip of land. When the French gave up on the continent, they left Thomas Jefferson with an offer too good to pass up. The War of 1812 was a reaction to lingering British designs on the continent, as was the Mexican War. If James Polk made a mistake, it was letting the defeated Santa Anna back into Mexico from his exile in Cuba. There, Santa Anna demagogued against America. A border dispute between Mexico and America led to the first shots of a war that would add the entire Southwest, from Texas to California, to the young nation. The 7,000 or so Mexicans of Spanish descent then living in California preferred American rule to Mexican. Still, the war represented another major land grab by the United States. More ominously, it forever altered the delicate population balance that existed in the republic's early years between the North and South. Going back further, the War of 1812 had its own baneful aftermath. The short conflict led to protectionist legislation in a vain attempt to pay for war costs. Such legislation, in turn, made the tariff issue a serious bone of contention between the two regions. Old Rightists eagerly subscribe to Charles Adams's thesis that the tariff was the reason for both the Deep South's secession and Abraham Lincoln's decision to go to war.[10]

And so, the War Between the States was a far more serious story. Here was the first great American catastrophe, the dividing line in American history, a war whose consequences led many conservatives to despair that the old Republic had been vanquished forever. Again, Bradford was a leading light on the revisionist front. He wasn't the first to criticize the Lincoln legacy, just the most accomplished. Bradford's Lincoln scholarship is not large (only a handful of essays), but it is sweeping—and, needless to say, it gained him a lasting notoriety among the conservative elite. Bradford attacked Lincoln on rhetorical and practical grounds. Like most Republicans, Lincoln rejected the abolitionists, but like those New Englanders, he often engaged in extreme flights of rhetoric. He was, in fact, the first true revolutionary to occupy the White House. Consider the Gettysburg Address. Calling for a "new birth of freedom" was one thing. Previous presidents were only happy to preserve the genuine birth of republican-style freedom won at Yorktown and Philadelphia. That was all the job entailed. At Gettysburg, Lincoln performed a sleight of hand by attempting to make the Declaration of Independence a governing document. Again, American presidents always understood that only the U.S. Constitution could be used for that purpose. Furthermore, the American nation was never imperiled by the secession of seven, sparsely populated states. Nor was self-government in danger of disappearing from the face of the earth; after all, it existed in numerous nations thousands of miles and oceans apart from America's shores. Prior to the Gettysburg Address, Lincoln's most damaging pronouncement was that the nation, nay, the world, must be "all one thing or all another." There's no room for dissent in such sentiments, no room for pluralism, or for distinct cultures to survive and flourish. Even conservatives such as Richard Weaver, who generally admired Lincoln, interpreted that single phrase as paving the way for the coming American empire. It could also serve as a guide for the totalitarian fanatics that defined the twentieth century.[11]

There was also Lincoln's handling of the war. He approved and encouraged the total war waged on Southern property and civilians by various federal armies. Here, in Bradford's view (and many others, including Lincoln's political opponents of the day), was an American-style tyranny. In one particularly stinging passage from Bradford's "The Lincoln Legacy: The Long View," the author charges that Lincoln's "tenure as dictator" began in April, 1861 with the summoning of a militia, the suspension of federal law (including the right of *habeas corpus*), military recruitment, a naval blockade of Southern ports, and the pledging of the nation's credit—all done while Congress was out of session. Throughout the war, Lincoln created both units of government "not known to the Constitution," including the state of West Virginia; he seized property in both the North and South; arrested thousands of political foes; shut down hundreds of adversary newspapers; interfered with duly elected state legislators (especially using federal troops to ensure a pro-Union victory in Maryland state elections); and finally, "employed the Federal hosts to secure his own reelection," an election where 38,000 votes cast the other way "might have produced an armistice and negotiated peace under a President McClellan."[12]

In our jaded world, the ends justify the means, but for Bradford, the Constitution was a sacred trust. Meanwhile, Lincoln would serve as the model many a future president would both envy and seek to emulate.

It is understandable that Bradford, whose ancestors wore the gray, would deliver such a devastating critique. What is notable is that well before Bradford, much of the criticism leveled at Lincoln came from Northern intellectuals: Edmund Wilson, Edgar Lee Masters, H. L. Mencken. Modern-day conservative critics of the sixteenth president were also from the Upper Sixteen, many of them descendants of European immigrants, with no familial roots in the 1860s America. Take the case of Frank S. Meyer, former communist *appartchik* and native of the industrial city of Newark, New Jersey, or Murray Rothbard, the New York City-born son of an iconoclastic Polish Jewish immigrant. For them, a legacy of the war was the rise of centralized power in a nation whose Founding Fathers held a dim view of an energetic, all-powerful national government. Meyer, for one, saw the Lincoln administration as the baneful predecessor to Franklin Roosevelt's New Deal. Such criticism held some currency during the vibrant conservative debates of the late 1950s. A damning critique came also from Joseph Sobran. American principles of self-government, even taken to the point of secession (which the young Lincoln himself endorsed as a congressman opposed to the Mexican War) were washed away, maybe forever, by the War Between the States. "There is no exit from the federal government's jurisdiction," Sobran lamented in a 1996 column, "no matter how badly it abuses or exceeds its constitutional powers. That is the ultimate meaning of 'Saving the Union.'"[13]

Not all conservatives, even those on the Old Right, would vilify Lincoln. Richard Weaver always claimed that Lincoln's "argument from definition," one based on individual freedom and reform according to law, was a good enough rhetorical model for conservatives to follow. Russell Kirk would champion Lincoln as a "common clay defender of order." Kirk acknowledged that Lincoln fought for union rather than abolition, that he wanted the freeman relocated in the West Indies or South America. Still, Lincoln was a president who would have practiced moderation in peacetime. The defeated South, if Lincoln had his way, would have been spared the horrors of reconstruction. Like Bradford, Andrew Lytle was highly critical of Lincoln's war policies, but he was also convinced that Lincoln's "malice toward none, charity towards all" stand, inspired by the learned horrors of a total war policy, was sincere, even though the running dogs of radical Republicanism would never allow that to happen. Such opinions, however, increasingly became minority ones. Lincoln, more than any nineteenth-century president, sent the nation down its wrong road from a republic to an aggressive superstate.[14]

Old habits die hard. Despite war and reconstruction, a considerable degree of statesmanship and republican virtues existed among both the ruling class and the public. By the late 1870s, Northern public opinion turned against the "plundering generation" running rampant in the now-supine South. In 1876, a conservative New York City Democrat, Samuel Tilden, received the majority of the popular vote in that year's presidential contest. Radical Republicans, however, controlled both houses of Congress. Not wanting to lose presidential power, the Republicans made a deal with Southern electors: Allow our candidate (Rutherford B. Hayes) to become president and we will withdraw all troops from Southern soil. Reconstruction ended, but the mighty fury of a national state had unleashed its wrath in a fearsome manner that Dickinson and Henry could have all-too-easily predicted.

The decades following the war were a period of some normalcy. The two regions went their own ways. The South remained agrarian. The famed New South orator, Henry Grady, championed an industrial order while also hoping the region would remain true to its political and religious traditions. Southerners agreed with Grady on cultural issues, but they would not yet see large-scale industrialism. Meanwhile, the confident, victorious North became more urban and prosperous. A few radical Republicans remained on the scene, but their influence had diminished considerably. The war was a great tragedy, reconstruction an embarrassment to the memory of the valorous soldiers who fought it. The idea (and practice) of local sovereignty remained central to the American character.

Pat Buchanan would herald this Republican Party-dominated era as an economic golden age. Not free trade, but a jealous protectionism catapulted America past Great Britain as the world's mightiest economic power. And as Buchanan liked to note, the two Republicans on Mount Rushmore—Abraham Lincoln and Theodore Roosevelt—were both avowed protectionists. "Thank God, I am not a free trader," remarked Roosevelt, as Great Britain, in 1908, surrendered her economic preeminence to the feisty upstart from across the ocean.[15]

Not only Lincoln and Roosevelt, but other Republicans, including William McKinley, William Howard Taft, Warren Harding, and Calvin Coolidge all rejected utopian notions of free trade and, in general, conducted successful domestic policies. According to Buchanan, protectionism allowed American industries to grow. But these Republicans were not "big-government conservatives." Tariffs, as critics on the right have long charged, did not mean a larger, more intrusive government. During the Coolidge years, government spending was cut to a mere 3 percent of the GNP, while taxes were also lowered. Throughout the early twentieth century, the GNP grew at a rate of 7 percent a year. For Buchanan, an economic nirvana had been achieved. "The factory did not replace the farm," he observed, "it was built alongside it." Into the 1970s, America remained an industrial and economic power.[16]

However, this economic golden age was marred by the descent into empire. The nineteenth century was a time of consolidation at home and empire-building abroad. The modern German nation was forged, as was the Italian one. The welfare state came into being. With the War Between the States, the question of secession in America was settled. Other nations now rose to challenge Great Britain's economic and military hegemony. The industrialized nations found empire-building too easy to pass up. It has long been said that the British Empire was a "mistake," a case of a powerful nation having its way by default with smaller, poorer ones.

Critics of the era from Rutherford B. Hayes to Franklin Roosevelt point to both the Spanish-American War and Woodrow Wilson's insistence that the United States enter World War I as proof that America was not immune from imperial sentiments. Motives behind the sinking of the *Maine*, the *casus belli* of the Spanish-American War has long been questioned by numerous historians. It was not intentional, rather simply a matter of an American ship hitting a mine. When war with Spain came, descendants of Johnny Reb joined those of Billy Yank to fight and easily defeat a decaying Spanish Empire on battlefields in

Cuba and the Philippines. President William McKinley, a son of small-town Ohio, had not wanted to go to war, but his cabinet, led by the demagogic young Theodore Roosevelt, put enormous pressure on him to fight the Spaniards. The yellow press whipped up public opinion and eventually, McKinley could not resist the war drums. The war left America with several thorny problems. The still-young republic now ruled and occupied foreign nations, including the large and populous Philippines. Young Americans were once again sent into the killing fields, this time to put down a bloody insurrection on that island archipelago. The Philippines was eventually granted independence. However, in the Caribbean, America refused to grant the same right to its holdings there, including Puerto Rico. One hundred years after the Spanish-American War, Republican leaders in Congress began a push to make Puerto Rico, a Spanish-speaking island of five million, mostly poor inhabitants, the fifty-first state. As if this is what America—with its mammoth problems of massive immigration, multiculturalism, and bilingual educational programs—really needed.

An earlier generation of Americans became disgusted with reconstruction. Likewise, an opposition force existed to counter the excesses of the Gilded Age. An Anti-Imperialist League was formed. Politicians and journalists joined in the chorus. "What are we going to get out of this war as a nation?" asked Georgia senator, Tom Watson, "Endless trouble, complications, expense. Republics cannot go into the conquering business and remain republics." Added William Graham Sumner, "If we believe in liberty...why do we not stand by it? Why are we going to throw it away and enter upon a Spanish policy of domination and regulation?" The famed industrialist, Andrew Carnegie, also opposed the war.[17]

The most eloquent anti-imperialist was William Jennings Bryan. The "Homer from the plains" wasn't perfect. Bryan, in fact, cynically voted for annexation of the Philippines following the war, believing that then *freeing* those islands would make a good campaign issue for the Democrats in 1900. Decades later, however, Bryan would be fondly hailed as the Old Right's politician of choice from the Gilded Age. Although he tried three times, Bryan never made it to the White House. Still, he articulated a Middle American populism that held great appeal to politicians both honest about such an approach and those who only faked it. A Midwesterner born to Southern parents, Bryan championed an "Alleghenies to the Rockies" patriotism that Willmoore Kendall, among others, took up with great gusto in the 1950s and 1960s. Bryan despised an East Coast elite that ruled the media, and urged on foreign wars. "[The] Allegheny Mountains are the salvation of the rest of the country," he claimed after resigning as Woodrow Wilson's secretary of state, "as they serve as a dike to keep the prejudice, the venom, the insolence, and the ignorance of the New York press from inundating the Mississippi valley."[18]

In short, Bryan's *style* was important to conservatives. His legacy was both symbolic and tactical, championing rural, small-town economies and cultures against numerous corrupting influences from the urban Northeast. "My friends, remember that relief cannot come to you from those who have fastened this yoke upon you," he thundered in a 1896 speech. "You may go to New York or Boston and find financiers...that know more about Europe than they do about the United States. They go oftener to London than to the great prairies of the West and South." In decades hence, numerous pundits and politicians would echo the same battle cry. Most pundits were sincere; politicians substantially less so. Still, Middle American values and anxieties will shape whatever future conservatism has. Where else will the revolution come from?[19]

Bryan's heirs had some real victories. When World War I broke out in 1914, the public had no desire for America's participation in that far-off conflict. American presidents were never thought of as world leaders. In 1916, Wilson was reelected president on an antiwar plank. However, in a second term, Wilson's utopian impulses also could not be checked. He began working to get America into the war. Several factors proved decisive. There were the ruling elites' deep Anglophile leanings, which only grew more intense as Britain's war with Germany became more precarious. There also were loans by top Wall Street banks to the Allies. If England lost the war, those American banks would find themselves in financial ruin. Plus, there was the dubious "Zimmerman telegraph" which had revealed German designs on Mexico. From there, the Kaiser's charges allegedly would foment revolution against the United States and liberate the Southwest for a resentful Mexico. Finally, there was German blundering. German U-boats constantly launched military attacks on American vessels, pushing America closer to a war her citizens did not want.

After the war, Wilson became the first U.S. president to visit Europe. With America established as an economic and possibly, a military power, Wilson launched his final crusade, this one for the League of Nations, where America and the victorious European powers would divide up the globe and herald a lasting peace. But Wilson faced a surprisingly strong opposition, one led by Idaho Senator William P. Borah. If Bryan was the voice of the Democratic Party's fading concern with a Jeffersonian agrarian order, then Borah represented Republican Party-style Americanism at its best. Borah could not be easily pigeonholed. Western states had a progressive streak in them and Borah supported foreign aid, Social Security, and woman's suffrage. But like Bryan, he was a forceful opponent of a budding American empire. In opposing the League of Nations, Borah joined forces with fellow senator, Henry Cabot Lodge and Alice Roosevelt Longworth, TR's colorful daughter, who claimed the League was contrary to her father's own politics. "Fa-tha," she asserted, would view American membership in the League as a "complete surrender of our independence as a nation."[20]

The League of Nations debate, at least temporarily, destroyed stereotypes of a stuffy GOP controlled by Wall Street bankers. From the West and Midwest, there came a strong and patriotic noninterventionism, a desire by Old Stock and immigrant populations alike to stay out of power plays by European nations that would inevitably bring the U.S. into conflict with Europe's global holdings. Great Britain's subjects, especially those in Asia, were becoming restless. "England has suggested (all England has to do now is to suggest) that we send 100,000 men to Constantinople," Borah told a Chicago audience during the great debate. If America enters the League, he added, they "*will* go, but without the consent of the American people." American troops would serve as bodyguards for an empire it once defeated to gain independence.[21]

Borah and others remained steadfast to George Washington's doctrine of no entangling alliances with foreign powers. Plus, they saw America as uniquely blessed. The continental-sized nation, happily separated from Europe and Asia by two large oceans, faced no military threat from abroad. Borah and his allies denounced this alien cult of internationalism, which often meant both bullying small countries for economic gain and engaging in quixotic crusades for a global democracy that most of the world's nations would reject anyway.

The Senate voted down American participation in the League of Nations. A Republican, Warren Harding succeeded Wilson, and the GOP's reign in the White House continued throughout the 1920s. Furthermore, the GOP finally responded to public pressure on another nation-defining issue. In 1924, the party, with help from some Democrats, enacted sharp restrictions on European immigration into America. Such legislation, which was also supported by AFL-CIO boss, Samuel

Gompers and black leaders as different as Booker T. Washington and
W. E. B. DuBois, was marked not only by economics, but by cultural
concerns as well. Since the offspring of European immigrants have
long assimilated into the nondescript suburban landscape of post-World
War II America, opposition to such immigration on cultural grounds
now seems strange, if not outright comical. But massive influxes of
Eastern, Central, and Southern European immigrants did, for many
decades, cause alarm to inhabitants of what was mostly a British, Prot-
estant nation. "Great in many ways, the United States is our land," said
Rep. Albert Johnson of California in a particularly poignant remark
following passage of immigration reform legislation. "If it is not the
land of our fathers, at least it may be, and should be, the land of our
children....The day of unalloyed welcome to all people...has definitely
ended."[22]

The League of Nations rejection and immigration restrictions drove
home the point that post-World War I America, tired and shocked by
the bloodshed of the Great War, was turning inward. Americans were
more concerned about cultural mores in their own increasingly urban
nation. In addition, many Americans now saw World War I as a conflict
only fought to save the East Coast bankers and their loans to the Allies.
That sentiment also contributed mightily to disillusionment over the
war.

And so, a conservatism existed in America during the 1920s. There
was, however, no "conservative movement," no journal like *National
Review* to lay down guidelines for proper behavior. The most celebrated
journalist of the age, H.L. Mencken, was properly antistatist. Indeed,
he has long been claimed by libertarians as one of their own. However,
Mencken was hampered by a boorish, knee-jerk dislike for any American president. He even skewered the genuinely conservative Calvin
Coolidge, a piece of demagoguery he later regretted. But traditionalists did not necessarily need the support of celebrity journalists. They
already had strong voices in the mass media. Both the highly popular
Saturday Evening Post and Colonel Robert McCormick's feisty *Chicago Tribune* enunciated traditionalist views in a bold, unapologetic
fashion. the *Post* especially championed a small-town way of life. Taking a stand against mass immigration, it fretted that America's population might someday reach two hundred million, "a truly ghastly number." Meanwhile, the *Tribune* celebrated "Chicagoland," a vast repose
of Midwestern values standing against the internationalists who dominated the political culture of the Northeast. Politically, traditionalists

had a decent foothold among both Midwestern and Western Republicans and states rights Southern Democrats. Unlike with the Republican Party of the 1970s, 1980s, and 1990s, an establishment that continually betrayed its constituencies, traditionalists could count on responsible leadership. That leadership, as an admiring Sam Francis recalls, gave full fidelity to the Constitution, the free enterprise system, and an America First foreign policy. "It was," Francis observed, "...a real class that had something to conserve, and it generally knew that it could not conserve it unless it also conserved the social and cultural fabric through which it exercised social power."[23]

The nation's founding agrarian culture stayed alive and well into the 1920s. The Northeast and Midwest were both dotted with large cities, but such entities remained an aberration. A healthy contrast of rural cultures and large, vibrant cities existed. The city was there as a refuge for a small-town lad from the South or Midwest to escape to and write their accounts, fictional or otherwise, of life back home. Numerous Americans artists, including Willa Cather, Eugene O'Neill, Thomas Wolfe, Theodore Dreiser, Edgar Lee Masters, Allen Tate, Caroline Gordon, and Sherwood Anderson, to name just a few, found a hospitable climate in New York City's Greenwich Village as a place to live and write about a traditional American culture far from the locale they toiled in. But directly outside the city limits, the countryside emerged. Novelists as different as Andrew Lytle and Saul Bellow have recalled an America where the frontier existed right on the doorstep of large cities.

2

The First Old Right

Common wisdom has always held that the Great Depression was exacerbated to the point of catastrophe by the 1930 Smoot-Hawley tariff legislation. In his acclaimed study of that era, *The Great Depression*, Murray Rothbard gave only a few paragraphs to Smoot-Hawley. For a libertarian such as Rothbard, Smoot-Hawley was a mistake, but it was not responsible for the Depression. Instead, that tragic era was part of a global disaster, sparked by runaway inflation resulting from reckless overlending by major banks in both Europe and America. Other villains included the unelected members of the Federal Reserve Board. The Fed, a creation of the Wilson administration, allowed the unwise credit expansion to take place. Rothbard took a dim view of much government intervention during the Depression. He also determined that many of President Hoover's policies were reasonable, whether they entailed the public sector or trying to rally the private sector to support the economy.[1]

Rothbard's friend, Pat Buchanan, went further on the subject of tariffs. The columnist scoffed at any notion that Smoot-Hawley extended the Depression. In response to criticism of his 1998 polemic against globalism, *The Great Betrayal*, Buchanan cited free trader Milton Friedman, who claimed that such protectionist legislation "played no significant role in either causing the Depression or prolonging it." Formulating his own analysis, Buchanan claimed, "When Smoot-Hawley was enacted in June 1930...U.S. imports were but four percent of GNP, and fully two-thirds of those came in duty-free. Can any economist seriously contend that a marginal tax hike on 1.3 percent of GNP can cause 25 percent unemployment, collapse 5,000 banks, wipe out five-sixths of all stock values and reduce GNP by 46 percent?"[2]

Agreeing with Rothbard, Buchanan claimed the Depression was caused by "the crash of a market whose prices had been inflated by an explosion of the money supply." This was compounded by a Federal Reserve Board which "failed to replenish the economy's lost blood as Hoover and FDR compounded the Fed's felony by tripling income-tax rates." Finally, to exonerate both the Federal Reserve Board and the Roosevelt administration, "free trade propagandists" made Smoot-Hawley their convenient scapegoat.[3]

Revisionism aside, the Depression brought down the Hoover administration and the Republican Party's era of presidential dominance. Nineteen thirty-two saw the election of Franklin D. Roosevelt and the rise of a new, more urban, more liberal Democratic Party. For the Old Right, Roosevelt, as much as Lincoln, stands as the president most responsible for centralizing power and destroying the foundations of the old Republic. Roosevelt did not always identify himself with government action. On the campaign trail in 1932, he railed against the deficit spending of the Hoover administration. Once in power, however, Roosevelt began priming the pump. Aided by solid Democratic majorities in both houses, the Roosevelt administration raced through its famous "100 days" revolution. In time, such massive federal spending programs as the Public Works Administration, the Civilian Conservation Corps, the Agricultural Adjustment Administration, and most importantly, the Social Security Act were duly debated, voted on, and signed into law. However, it was the creation of the National Recovery Administration (NRA) that got the anti-New Dealers on the offensive.

Some of FDR's mightiest critics, including Senator Borah and Colonel Robert McCormick, actually supported early New Deal initiatives, such as cutting the size of the Federal workforce. However, the NRA was another matter. The New Dealers, like modern-day Tom Paines, were determined to "make the world over." With the NRA, trade associations would set the terms of prices, wages, and products. There were even attempts to control the media, in those days dominated by newspapers. NRA Chief General Hugh Johnson hailed his agency as "the new constitution of the United States." Restrictions on the First Amendment got Colonel McCormick's dander up. His broadsides against such provisions forced FDR to quietly delete the media restriction clause. But while the NRA has disappeared into the history books, its legacy lives on: not just expanding the size and power of Washington, but the New Dealers' belief that the emergency of the Depression gave them the moral right to assault the Constitution, a document that, after all, was adopted way back in 1787. Whenever some New Dealers worried about the constitutionality of their programs, others would shrug it off, joking that "they weren't in Philadelphia." Such arrogance has never subsided among the power elites.[4]

There was little opposition to the Social Security Act of 1934. When Social Security was inaugurated, the average life expectancy in America was sixty-five, the same age as when benefits first kicked in. Furthermore, in the 1930s, there were forty-three taxpayers for every Social Security recipient. It didn't seem like much of a gamble. Still, Social Security, not the NRA, would become the crown jewel of the New Deal. Standing for a middle-class welfare state, the Democratic Party created and sustained a class of dependencies, new voting blocs that expected generous Social Security benefits once their working days were over. For conservatives, Social Security was the most revolutionary piece of economic legislation in American history. Now, a once-free people were forever hooked to the cradle-to-grave welfare state. Efforts to slowly replace Social Security through privatization, has for decades, been a leading conservative reform project.

Roosevelt's economic agenda eventually ran into legal roadblocks. In the late 1930s, the Supreme Court shot down important New Deal legislation, such as the NRA, as being unconstitutional. Roosevelt didn't take it lying down. He went on the warpath, demagoging against the supposedly demented "nine old men" on the court. Not enough of these old boys would quit, so FDR embarked on his ambitious "court packing" crusade. He campaigned for legislation to increase the size of the court from nine to eleven justices. Hence, Roosevelt would not have to wait for justices to resign or die. He could appoint two new ones, hopefully swinging the court's majority his way.

The plan proved both highly controversial and unpopular. The U.S. Senate didn't like this bold power play at all. Even FDR's first-term vice president, John Nance Garner of Texas, was disdainful of the whole idea. Vice presidents were different figures in those pre-television days. Few people considered them would-be presidents. Garner, in fact, never gave a public speech during his entire time on the job. But he often signaled his displeasure with the boss by flying off to Texas unannounced. During the court-packing debate, he showed his hand by turning to his former Senate colleagues where he would "make a face" and give a thumbs down gesture.[5]

Despite heavy lobbying by FDR, the court packing legislation was defeated; a disaster compounded by large GOP gains in the 1938 midterm elections. Worse yet, the American economy remained in desperate straits. New Deal programs were an unmitigated failure. After six years of increased domestic spending, unemployment remained about the same as during the dark days of the early 1930s. In 1932, 11,586,000 Americans were out of work. By 1939, that number stood virtually stagnant at 11,369,000. "No one tells me what to do," an anguished President Roosevelt blurted out to the press. Government spending and progressive taxation proved to be no panacea for this worldwide depression.[6]

Still, New Deal opponents were up against a most skillful politician. Roosevelt was the first president to master the mass media, in this case, radio, one of which was placed in millions of American living rooms. Roosevelt's weekly fireside chats projected the image of a warm, benevolent leader. A politician who had taken his lumps (he was the vice presidential nominee on the Democrats' losing 1920 ticket), Roosevelt used populist rhetoric to overcome his Hyde Park aristocratic lineage. He especially enjoyed sailing into the "economic royalists" both on Wall Street and in the Republican Party in order to reach the poor and working classes in Middle America.

Moreover, Roosevelt did not waste any opportunities to shape the nation as he saw fit. His Supreme Court nominees were part of the mix. Conservative editorialists railed against Hugo Black, FDR's first High Court nominee, as a man who "treats the Constitution like a heifer." While Black had to publicly repudiate his former membership in the Alabama Ku Klux Klan, a Democratic majority in the Senate made his confirmation a sure thing. Black's nomination merely represented the first shot in a long battle. During FDR's long tenure, other liberal jurists, including Felix Frankfurter, William O. Douglas, and Robert H. Jackson would join Justice Black on the bench. As it turned out, expanding the court's membership ranks wasn't necessary.

New Dealers sought to manipulate American culture as well. Through various federally funded "arts projects," poets, novelists, and composers were enlisted in the cause of creating a "New Deal art," one that glorified spending programs designed to employ and uplift the working man. Works of drama, poetry, and biography that were either homages to the New Deal or written by pro-New Deal artists won Pulitzer Prizes—Robert Sherwood's biography of Roosevelt and Harry Hopkins, and Archibald MacLeish's book-length narrative poem, *Conquistador* being two examples. Liberals *do* take care of their own.[7]

The conservative establishment that flourished during the 1920s now found itself out of power. Yet, it became a spirited opposition. The mere philosophy of the New Deal—that a centralized, all-powerful regime can "control" the economy and society in general—created what Murray Rothbard called "the first old right." The opposition, mostly rural Midwesterners and Westerners, were a feisty bunch. Rothbard fondly reflected on voting records by Midwestern Republicans that "make most right-wing congressmen today seem impossibly leftist and socialistic." Rothbard also recalled the ideological diversity of the loosely defined opposition. There were, for instance, disagreements on trade, immigration, and a foreign policy that best served American interests. Some anti-New Dealers wanted to repeal not just FDR's revolution, but all "progressive" legislation of the late-nineteenth and early-twentieth centuries. Still, nothing prevented the group from focusing on its main goal: Stopping the Roosevelt administration's drive for consolidation of all power in the Federal city.[8]

The opposition boasted such diverse stylists as H.L. Mencken, Garet Garret, Rose Wilder Lane, Isabel Paterson, Albert Jay Nock, and John T. Flynn. In the 1930s, Mencken's reputation remained solid, while Garret was an important contributor to the *Saturday Evening Post*. Flynn labored in the highly competitive world of New York journalism, while also writing a regular column for the *New Republic*, the premier pro-New Deal journal of its day.

Paleos have claimed these writers as intellectual forebears. Mencken, Garret, and Nock were all fierce individualists. New Deal planning, they feared, would turn Americans into mere serfs of the state. There was also the idea of America as a nation of communities. A lyrical opposition to twentieth century statism came from the Vanderbilt Agrarians, most notably in their 1930 manifesto, *I'll Stand My Stand*. The Agrarians included paleo favorites Donald Davidson, Andrew Lytle, and the historian Frank Owsley, plus other, more famous men of letters as John Crowe Ransom, Robert Penn Warren, and Allen Tate. The Agrarians first came together as poets at Vanderbilt, eventually publishing a well-received modernist journal, the *Fugitive*. The Scopes Monkey Trial, with its global condemnation of the South's "backward" Christian fundamentalism, drove the Fugitives into a more polemical stance, which soon included the burning question of whether the South should fully embrace the cult of industrialism. The introduction to *Stand,* written mostly by John Crowe Ransom, hammered industrialism on both economic and cultural grounds, but it was the latter argument that remains most compelling. Some light industrialism, (i.e., small factories manned by craftsmen) was acceptable, but one that created a mass society was not. The "amenities of life," including "manners, conversation, hospitality, sympathy, family life, [and] romantic love" all suffered in a "strictly business" civilization. In this seminal collection, the South was urged by its brightest sons to stay true to its agrarian roots.[9]

Who Owns America?, the follow-up to *Stand*, was published in 1936 and faintly hoped to influence that year's elections. More prosaic than the previous volume, *Who Owns America?* nonetheless is representative of the opposition party. New Deal opposition was strongly Jeffersonian. Jefferson the agrarian, the states' rights man, the opponent of big government (while president, he cut the size of the federal government by 30 percent) remained the towering model of proper statesmanship. Anti-New Dealers liked both Jefferson's small-government stand and his vision of farmers and small landowners as constituting the foundation of American-style liberty.

The Agrarians brief foray into politics was a failure. Influenced by the British Distributionists, whose numbers included G.K. Chesterton and Hillaire Belloc, the Agrarians were not against some federal programs, at least those that might help keep beleaguered farmers on the land. A few Southern Democrats listened, but by the mid-1930s, New Deal-style statism seemed like the only solution to the Depression. In fact, it looked quite benign next to the Stalinist and Trotskyite elements on some American college campuses. Furthermore, the administration at Vanderbilt was hostile to the Agrarians. The young Robert Penn Warren, due to pressure from the Vanderbilt English Department, was denied even a night teaching job at a small college in Nashville. An overworked John Crowe Ransom would soon take a position at Kenyon College in Ohio. Davidson was the lone holdout, but he remained an optimist. He held out hope for some political gain. He also saw the rise of regionalism in the arts as a healthy rebellion from Middle America. His 1938 classic, *The Attack on Leviathan*, championed the regional cultures of the Middle West, the Far West, the South, and New England. The Golden Age of American literature, begun in earnest during the 1920s, continued into the next decade. Davidson's examples of regionalists in literature included poets Edwin Arlington Robinson, Robert Frost, Edgar Lee Masters, and Vachel Lindsay, plus such novelists as Ellen Glasgow and William Faulkner, and painters Grant Wood and Thomas Hart Benton. Literature on the pages of the *American Review,* the *Southern Review,* the *Southwestern Review, American Prefaces,* the *Frontier* and the *Midland*, plus the "great Catholic movement for restoring rural life" defined a regionalism that was "anti-cosmopolitan, anti-monopolistic...[with] the consensus of the ideas [favoring] the growing tendency toward regional autonomy." [10]

A vibrant regionalism also served as a bulwark against the cultural fads coming from New York City, an entity that Davidson dismissed as a "world city," one not only woefully out of touch with the rest of America, but one that had also embraced the worst aspects of European decadence: Marxian theories of class warfare, Freudian doctrines of "repressions and complexes," German Expressionism, French Dadaism, plus the works of such alienated artists as D.H. Lawrence and James Joyce. The Tennessean himself was central to this counter-revolution. Such Davidson poems as "The Tall Men," as with those by Robert Frost, attempted to create a useable past, one that would offer a vision of the old American character to jaded modern audiences. Echoing Bryan, Davidson saluted the "old folks at home" in rural America. "Worn out with abstraction and novelty, plagued by divided counsel," such citizens, Davidson wrote in his essay, "The Diversity of America," "attach themselves—or re-attach themselves—to a home-section....They seek spiritual and cultural autonomy....They seek to define the nation in terms of its real and permanent rather than its superficial and temporary qualities. They are learning how to meet the subtlest and most dangerous foe of humanity—the tyranny that wears the mask of humanitarianism and benevolence. They are attacking Leviathan."[11]

The anti-New Deal right left many important legacies. Much of what they did would inform the more disciplined postwar right. Opposition to "social spending" policies are de riguer for our times, but the first Old Right made antistatism intellectually respectable. The New Deal, as much as the fanaticism gathering strength in Europe was, for the Old Right, about complete state control. In his 1940 book, *The Managerial Revolution*, James Burnham had no difficulty in placing communism, fascism, and the New Deal in similar categories. All three, for instance, relied heavily on large, impersonal bureaucracies. State planning, micromangement of economies, and the loss of sovereignty brought about by a transfer of power from the legislator to bureaucrats and judges also defined revolutions taking place in many Western nations. The entire criticism of a planned economy reached fruition with Friedrich Hayek's 1945 classic, *The Road to Serfdom*. Hayek's thesis, that such economies would also wipe out individual freedoms, was well anticipated by the hardy opposition movement of the 1930s.

Late in that decade, the world scene shifted dramatically, allowing Roosevelt to take on a different persona. "Dr. New Deal" would soon be replaced by "Dr. Win the War." While it is hard for later generations of Americans to imagine such a situation, the United States was not always a world power. Britain and France had their colonial holdings and strong militaries; the American people happily accepted the status quo on such world power matters. A military alliance between Britain and France, one proposed by the latter nation in the mid-1930s, might have checked Hitler's ambitions. By the end of the 1930s, however, that opportunity had come and gone. And so, with Europe under siege from German armies, the debate over America's entry into World War II became one of the most acrimonious in the nation's history. Consider only the exchange that took place between Roosevelt and Senator Burton Wheeler (D-Wyoming) in response to FDR's Lend Lease proposal. Under such a law, the president would be able to supply munitions to Great Britain without first receiving congressional approval. The plan, Senator Wheeler thundered, was "the New Deal's 'triple A' foreign policy—it will plow under every fourth American boy." That broadside, a flustered Roosevelt countered, was "the most untruthful...[the] most dastardly, unpatriotic thing that has ever been said....That really is the rottenest thing that has been said in public life in my lifetime."[12]

Opponents of Roosevelt's economic program soon found themselves against any war plans coming from Washington. "[Entry] into large-scale war," Rothbard recalled, "especially for global...concerns, would plunge America into a permanent garrison state that would wreck American liberty and constitutional limits at home even as it extended the American imperium abroad." For Flynn and Charles Beard, Roosevelt's maneuvering into the war was a diversion from the economic failure of the New Deal. The public, by large margins, was against American involvement in the European conflict. In 1940, both Roosevelt and his Republican Party rival, Wendell Wilkie, promised to keep the nation out of war. Neither man was telling the truth. By then, both were convinced that American military action would be necessary in both Europe and Asia to stop the Axis powers. At the 1940 Atlantic Conference with Great Britain, Roosevelt confided to Churchill that he needed an "incident" to get America into the war. The great debate was already underway. It was very much an East Coast vs. Midwest/Far West showdown. The more cosmopolitan Northeast leaned toward interventionism, while the Midwest, influenced by the *Chicago Tribune*, sounded the antiwar trumpet. The South, still poor and completely Democratic, sided with the mostly Democratic Northeast. Southerners prided themselves on seeing the threat posed by Hitler before, apparently, the rest of the country did. But such an alliance would have unforeseen consequences for the region. The war, as it turned out, allowed Washington to accumulate the power needed to prosecute a second reconstruction against their wartime allies below the Mason-Dixon line.[13]

On the Atlantic front, anti-interventionists held the upper hand, fighting passage of Roosevelt's Lend Lease program. The president's opponents attacked Lend Lease as not only a blank check for war action, but as a bill that would give dictatorial powers to the president. Anti-New Dealers, including Senators Borah, Wheeler, Gerald Nye, plus proponents of the popular America First Committee were not the "isolationists" their critics have long claimed they were. America First members favored a strong military, including increases in defense outlays. General George Marshall, chairman of the Joints Chief of Staff, publicly praised Congress for approving such a spending policy. Many senators also supported military aid to Great Britain, and, after it was invaded by Germany, to Russia as well. This would be enough to turn the tide, especially in Eastern Europe where Hitler had blundered badly by trying to take on the determined defenders of Mother Russia. However, all military aid would be in accordance with the Constitution, authorized by Congress and Congress alone. [14]

Frustrated in the Atlantic theater, Roosevelt, in 1940, performed his own rhetorical sleight of hand. He promised to keep American boys out of European wars. That was all. And so, after the election, the administration turned their sights on Asia. In the Pacific theater, the New Dealers opted for economic sanctions against Japan. The Japanese had invaded China in 1931, and would later form an alliance with Germany and Italy. For Herbert Hoover, who remained a strong opponent of his victorious rival, any military confrontation with Japan was foolish and unnecessary. The Japanese, he claimed, posed no military threat to the United States. Furthermore, they could never "Japantify" China, an ancient nation with thousands of years of tradition to cling to. Still, Japan is where the war came. Beard's revision, seconded by many Roosevelt critics, was particularly damning. Beard blamed Roosevelt's economic sanctions, especially an oil embargo on Japan, for pushing the latter into war. U.S. sanctions, Beard claimed, produced an "ultimate showdown" with the Japanese. Such sanctions *and* Pearl Harbor were both "mutually antagonistic acts." The New Dealers were "seeking" war, "maneuvering" Japan into war and the Land of the Rising Sun obliged them.[15]

When the war came, many anti-New Deal senators stayed on the offensive. Needless to say, it was a losing battle. Even Joe Sobran, a thorough FDR critic, notes that Congress did declare war on both Japan and later on Germany, thus making America's involvement legal in the eyes of the Constitution. The *Chicago Tribune* continued to oppose the administration, but the other big mass media gun of the Old Right, the *Saturday Evening Post*, caved in. The *Post* soon became pro-war, dropping Garret's column in the process. He wasn't the only victim. H.L. Mencken saw his once-gaudy reputation decline during the war years. As also was the case with John T. Flynn. Flynn was a registered Democrat, an old-fashioned anti-big government, pro-capitalist New Englander. Far from being new, FDR's exercise in government spending, money borrowing, and a war economy was in fact, an "old racket," a power grab practiced by despots throughout the ages. One 1940 Flynn essay in the *Yale Review* was so critical that Roosevelt himself took action. The president personally "suggested" that Flynn be censored not only from the *Yale Review*, but all other reputable journals of opinion. Which is what happened. Flynn eventually lost his column at the *New Republic*. In addition, many leading antiwar politicians retired, died, or were defeated at the polls. Some, especially Senator Wheeler, were victims of nasty smear campaigns. A 1947 book, *The Plot Against America*, by one "Daniel George Kin" depicted the senator as an out-and-out traitor. Wheeler bitterly protested the hit job on the Senate floor, but it was too late to prevent his reelection defeat.[16]

In 1997, an FDR monument was finally unveiled in Washington, D.C. Both Joe Sobran and Pat Buchanan strongly criticized the canonization of FDR, with Sobran proclaiming that Americans ought to "hang their heads in shame" at such a tribute. Granted that Roosevelt, by 1940 and the fall of France, had wanted America to enter the war. If so, then FDR, as Buchanan argued, should at least have had the "guts" to say so to the public rather than lying or dealing in semantics. This definitely was the minority view among Washington punditry. Conservatives had long adopted FDR as one of their own. The only controversy was whether the sculpture should depict FDR with his trademark cigarette holder or not. Fearless opponents of political correctness, conservatives supported the monument, but thought the smoker it honored should be portrayed as such.

The case against Roosevelt is a long one, and it still reverberates among the precincts of the Old Right. Most obvious is an economic revolution, the triumph of socialism in America. New Dealers claimed their measures were only "temporary" but conservatives have long learned that no government program is ever that way. They just grow and grow, taking on a life of their own, until no one questions their existence. As important were Roosevelt's activist justices, men who made hash of the tenth amendment, launching, in the process, a social revolution against long held American mores and values, an upheaval which remains in full motion.

Over half a century after World War II, there was still bitterness over the way FDR fought the war—and lost the peace. Russell Kirk and Richard Weaver were among the many critics of the firebombing of Dresden near the end of the war, an action which killed anywhere from 35,000 to 135,00 German civilians, most of them women and children. Winston Churchill's administration had fomented the raids, but they took place with American support and participation. For Weaver, the total war prosecuted not only by the Axis, but also by the Allies, represented one of those extreme actions which obliterated the restraining elements on which all civilized life is based. Indiscriminate warfare had occurred during the war between the states, and now the U.S. government was repeating the same mistake eighty years later.[17]

FDR's alliance with Joseph Stalin sealed the right's criticism. Most egregious was the sell-out of the ten Christian nations of Eastern Europe to Stalin's wolves. By 1945, Stalin's troops had already occupied Poland and other Eastern European nations. All FDR could do was accept lame promises of "free elections" by Stalin for those countries. Or so FDR apologists have long argued. Not true, countered several leading Old Rightists. Buchanan, Henry Regnery, and Robert Nisbet have all pointed out that FDR and Churchill practiced appeasement as early as 1943 at the Teheran conference. Rather than invading Europe through the "soft underbelly" of the Balkans (as Churchill had hoped for), FDR opted for the bloody land invasion of France. Why? As Sobran claims, neither FDR nor General George Marshall wanted to offend their new ally in the Kremlin, a man who already had designs on first, Eastern Europe, and then the rest of the continent. Such an alliance was doomed from the start. The Kremlin only entered the war effort as long as its dominance over the Baltics and Finland would remain intact. Allied war plans made in Teheran allowed Stalin to consolidate gains already achieved in Eastern Europe, making the appeasement at

Yalta a mere formality. At Teheran, Churchill even offered Stalin the German city of Konigsberg so as to satisfy Moscow's demand for a warm-water port.[18]

Great wars always change the nations and societies involved, usually in catastrophic fashion. Even the winning side is affected. This was especially true for World War II, a global conflict without precedent. Here was the first war in history to see massive killings of civilian populations. While the losers suffered foreign occupation, the victors paid a heavy price for their triumph. Great Britain lost her global predominance for good. Once masters of the sea, it was now both a second-rate military and economic player on the world scene. Along with Britain, nearly all of Western Europe would be placed under an American protectorate. While America basically provided for Western Europe's defense, such nations continued expanding their debilitating domestic welfare states. A hardy individualism was disappearing from the European scene. Furthermore, the postwar world saw not just a decades-long Cold War, but headaches galore for the old colonial powers: Portugal with Angola; Belgium and the Congo; Britain and India; and France with its bloody wars in Algeria and Vietnam—the latter a name soon all-too-familiar to working-class American boys. Suddenly subjects of the rising American empire, the British were pretty much forced to dismantle their empire, all over the protestations of Churchill, the man who once reveled in America's entry into the war.

For the Old Right, World War II meant the passing of an era, a way of life gone forever. Most eloquent was Harry Elmer Barnes who bluntly termed December 7, 1941 as "the end of the old America." Old Right criticism of the war can sound churlish: After all, American involvement *did* guarantee the eventual defeat of global fascism. But as noted, anti-interventionists were confident that Great Britain and Russia, with "all-out" congressionally approved American military aid could roll back Hitler's empire. Modern-day conservatives would utterly reject this contention. Conservatives have long repudiated the anti-interventionist right. They view them as, at best, a huge embarrassment to the cause. The 1990s Old Right, on the other hand, saw redeeming qualities from an America First foreign policy. Younger paleos such as Bill Kauffman and Justin Raimondo have found plenty of good things to say about the anti-interventionists. In the December 1991 *Chronicles*, surviving America First members were given space to recall that tumultuous era. Far from being "traitors," America Firsters were patriots who stood for both a strong defense and against needless interventionism. The new Old Right viewed such thinking as a sound enough lode-star for the post-Cold War era.[19]

Meanwhile, Mr. Barnes was proved correct. A new America was emerging from the war, one that would make conservatives feel even more like strangers in their own country. America won the war, but it was losing its civilization. Both Andrew Lytle and Wendell Berry have long circled 1940 as one of those fateful dates in American history. In that year, six million American families lived on their own farmland. The Jeffersonian ideal was still going strong. Twenty-five years later, those numbers had plummeted to just two million family farms. A full 62 percent of such family units had been lost. During the war, millions of Americans streamed into cities, looking for war-related jobs.[20] That was followed by the flight from the city to newly constructed suburban housing tracts, themselves soon to become the symbol of American living. The old civilizing balance between the small town and the big city was breaking down even more.

3

Cold War Conservatism

With the war over, it was back to the business of dismantling the New Deal. For a while, things were heading in that direction. The statism of the 1930s and 1940s was under some popular siege. As in the years after World War I, Americans were tired of war, tired of living in a garrison state. There was great domestic pressure on the government to bring the troops home, to have young fathers reunited with their families. In addition, Americans were weary of Democratic Party rule. In 1946, the Republicans regained control of both houses of Congress, while an unpopular Harry Truman was seen as a sure loser in the 1948 elections.

However, blunders at Teheran and Yalta were coming back to haunt the nation. With Poland in tow, Stalin reached for more conquests. Nineteen forty-seven saw Czechoslovakia go under. Moscow-supported coups also occurred in Hungary, Romania, and Bulgaria. A bipartisan congressional coalition approved military aid for Greece when that ancient nation was under assault from a Soviet-financed insurgency. The CIA, in 1950, helped to engineer the defeat of Italian communists who appeared to be heading toward victory at the polls. But by then, the conflict was in full gear. In 1949, Mao Tse-Tung's "agrarian reformers" completed their long march to power. Winston Churchill's famous Iron Curtain speech in Fulton, Missouri was intended to wake up a fatigued American public. One forgets that Churchill couched the struggle in cultural terms, defending Europe's "Christian nations" against Stalinite totalitarianism. Either way, the welfare-warfare state was back in business.

The leader for the Old Right was now Robert A. Taft, son of the former president, senior senator from Ohio, and a politician who steadfastly ignored the "conservative" label. When a journalist once asked

Taft if he had read Russell Kirk's *The Conservative Mind*, the senator replied in the negative and quipped, "you remind me of Thurber's *Let Your Mind Alone*." Murray Rothbard remembered Taft as a brilliant man who nonetheless was too philosophically devoted to compromise.[1]

Taft's anti-New Deal stand soon translated into opposition to the incipient North Atlantic Treaty Organization (NATO) alliance. With NATO, the United States, unlike after World War I, would now remain in Europe. Taft would use American air power to defend Europe, but he opposed the idea of ground troops permanently stationed on that continent. Taft was no isolationist. His anticommunism included beefing up the American presence in Asia. But he knew that a global military empire would keep the U.S. safe for New Deal-style socialism.

Taft's anti-interventionism earned him plenty of enemies among the Wall Street money boys who pretty much called the shots within the Republican Party. In 1948, the Republicans nominated New York governor and celebrated crime-buster, Thomas Dewey, a man who had earlier lost to FDR in 1944. Dewey, as any Chicago journalist knows, sat on a big lead the polls gave him over Truman in the 1948 presidential election. The campaign was a classic match-up between a feisty, Middle America Democrat who employed populist sentiments against an East Coast Republican only distinguished by fidelity to "good government."

Despite this embarrassment, the Wall Street elites were in no mood to see a foe of an emerging globalism receive their party's presidential standard. Luckily for them, World War II hero Dwight D. Eisenhower, after mulling things over, decided to run for president as a Republican rather than a Democrat. (He could have easily served in either party.) In 1952, the presidential nomination contest was far different from today's front-loaded primary process, where Southern, Midwestern, and Western states all lump their primaries together on single days. There was New Hampshire and only a handful of other primaries. The action took place at the convention, where state chairmen, big-city bosses, union leaders, influential senators, governors, and representatives of the big-moneyed interests swung state delegations around to their candidates-of-choice. "Old Right Republicans... always managed to lose the presidential nomination," Rothbard recalled. "[The] Eastern Establishment-Big Banker-Rockefeller wing of the party...used their media clout, as well as hardball banker threats to call in the delegates' loans, to defeat majority sentiment in the party."[2]

Eisenhower prevailed over Taft in 1952, causing the Ohioan's bitter remark that since 1932 "every GOP nomination has been controlled by

Chase Manhattan Bank." Oddly enough, Eisenhower shared Taft's mis-
trust of NATO. In addition, he strongly opposed American military
action on the Asian continent, promising, if elected, to end the Korean
War and later on, lecturing on the folly of an American land war in
Vietnam. Ike supported NATO, but he also insisted that this was only a
temporary affair. In ten years time, by the end of the 1950s, the free
European states would be back on their feet economically, industrial
giants once again. A newly prosperous Europe could easily be able to
pay for its own defense against the Soviet threat. America would then
pack up and go home, while still remaining allies with nations of Western Europe.

It didn't work out that way, as a popular President Eisenhower saw
himself pitifully overruled by his own State Department on the NATO
question. A memorable scene from Bill Kauffman's *America First!* il-
lustrates Ike's rude introduction to the realities of empire. While
Eisenhower declared that it was "our policy" to begin reducing American troop size in Europe, both Secretary of State John Foster Dulles
and top presidential aide, Andrew Goodpaster, begged to differ, claiming that it was actually a vague "long-term" goal, one only possible
when the Europeans filled the military gap created by the Americans'
departure. Since that gap, presumably, could never be filled, the troops
remained at present levels all over the commander-in-chief's insistence
that they start coming home.[3]

The first Old Right was a victim of Cold War politics. For Murray
Rothbard, the main intellectual culprit was William F. Buckley, Jr. and
the founding of the latter's *National Review*. While Rothbard admitted
that *NR*, which published its first issue in 1955, was lively and well
edited, it started, under the banner of anticommunism, the right's lurch
toward internationalism and statism. During the 1950s, Rothbard occasionally wrote for *NR*. He only cut off his association with the
Buckleyites in 1962, after a soon-to-be-famous disagreement over the
privatization of federally managed lighthouses. Buckley considered
Rothbard's idea an eccentric irrelevancy. For Rothbard, the argument
represented a culmination of differences between Buckley and himself, and he no longer wrote for *NR*.

Rothbard was correct in his assessment of *National Review's* early
style. It was a blast of bold, fresh thinking on a right front grown crabby
and defeatist under years of Democratic Party rule. In addition to being a prolific writer, Buckley was articulate, witty, and telegenic. Here
was a learned conservative made for the television age. Buckley was a

"cool" performer in a "hot" medium. Displaying many of the same gifts that rocketed Ronald Reagan to political power, Buckley was a frequent guest on numerous television programs, from *Meet the Press* to *The Jack Paar Show*, before eventually hosting his own one-hour talk show, the award-winning *Firing Line*. "[With] his quasi-aristo-cratic English public-school bearing, his fearsome knowledgeability, and his devastating wit...[one] was confronted with a persona that the liberalism of the 1950s was hard put to match," an admiring William Rusher recalled.[4]

For the editors of *National Review*, the 1950s were a romp, a time for an unabashedly conservative journal to slay sacred cows and have fun doing so. The publication soon established itself as the premier journal on the right for a mid-1950s nation of 150 million people. In its inaugural issue, the editors boldly claimed the publication would "stand athwart history, yelling stop." It would both arrest the retreat of the West in the face of Soviet communism abroad and turn back the trend toward statism at home, while also reaffirming ancient Judeo-Christian values. Circulation inched toward 30,000 by 1960, but the real fun had to be in *NR's* standing as an irreverent, but intellectual publication going up against no less than eight liberal weeklies. Plus, Buckley had garnered real talent: James Burnham, Frank S. Meyer, Richard Weaver, Willmoore Kendall, John S. Chamberlain, John Dos Passos, Whittaker Chambers, Henry Hazlitt, and Russell Kirk were among the journal's early senior editors and regular contributors. Kirk and Weaver, mean-while, eloquently articulated an antimaterialistic, antimodernist vision for conservatives. These two, in particular, have remained Old Right favorites.

Weaver's first published work, *Ideas Have Consequences*, took up cudgels against an urban society where the terminally spoiled masses were kept prostrate by political demagogues promising "the best of everything," a sensationalist media that presented a bleak and false view of life, and their own rootless existence. As with the Vanderbilt Agrarians, Weaver preferred the rural man who inhabits a world "where memories live longer" and where "what his grandfather did was real to him." Weaver's prescription for renewal included a return to private property, truth in the written and spoken word, and an emphasis on piety. Quoting Plato, Weaver championed a world where parents would bequeath to their children "not riches, but the spirit of reverence." Though bitterly attacked in the liberal press, *Ideas* was hailed by conservatives and traditionalists, including Kendall, John Crowe Ransom,

and Cleanth Brooks, plus even Reinhold Niebuhr, the influential liberal theologian. More importantly, Weaver's program of restoration
would serve as inspiration for Frank Meyer's fusionist platform to unite
libertarians and traditionalists into a cultural and political force.[5]

Ideas Have Consequences was published in 1948. The book's importance was matched and eventually eclipsed by Russell Kirk's 1953 opus,
The Conservative Mind. By the 1950s, it was generally agreed by all that
America's intellectual tradition, springing forth from Thomas Jefferson's
Declaration of Independence and the U.S. Constitution's Bill of Rights,
was solidly liberal. The Lockean notion that man was a blank slate who
could be shaped into perfection by state action reigned supreme. Secular
democracy, equality of results, a capitalism buttressed by state spending,
and the cult of strong presidents were the American creeds.

Kirk came along to say that wasn't necessarily so. The Anglo-Ameri-
can tradition, from Edmund Burke to John Adams, from John C.
Calhoun to Benjamin Disraeli, and finally, from George Santayana to
T. S. Eliot, was, in fact, deeply conservative. It put no faith in democracy as a saving god; it had no use for socialism or planned economies;
however, it would not let an unfettered, predatory capitalism define its
heritage, either. While Weaver hailed the "nonmaterialistic society" of
the Old South, Kirk championed the "unbought grace of life" as articulated by Edmund Burke. Social classes, a responsible hierarchy, prudent reform (when necessary), a decentralized government, and those
"little platoons" of family, church and neighborhood, were among the
tenets that Kirk hoped would come to define American conservatism.

Kirk's book received a remarkable stroke of luck. Today, middlebrow publications such as *Time* and *Newsweek* publish, if at all, only
skimpy book reviews. In 1953, however, Kirk was aided tremendously
by the presence of Whittaker Chambers, who then served as a senior
editor at *Time*. Chambers considered *The Conservative Mind* to be "one
of the most important books that is likely to appear in some time." As
such, he pushed for a full-length review of the book. As it turned out,
the entire book review section of the July 6, 1953 *Time* was devoted to
a positive review of *The Conservative Mind*. Numerous other reviews
and essays in both large-circulation newspapers and smaller-circula-
tion journals of opinion followed. The *Partisan Review*, for instance,
published not one, but two lengthy reviews. Both Kirk, his publisher,
Henry Regnery, and modern American conservatism itself had arrived.[6]

It was also a stroke of good fortune that Eisenhower was in power
when *National Review* took off. The Buckleyites had fun tweaking a

popular GOP president, whom they deemed insufficiently anticommunist. Such a stand solidified *NR's* iconoclastic reputation. It also served
notice that conservatives would not be placated just because a Republican was in the White House. The Eisenhower administration spent
too much money; Ike even vetoed tight budgets passed by a Democratic congress. More serious was Eisenhower's foreign policy. In June
1956, British, French, and Israeli forces attacked Egypt's Suez Canal,
a British-owned entity recently nationalized by the Egyptian ruler,
Gamal Nassar. However, Eisenhower gave no support to America's traditional allies. He lowered the boom on the British, forcing a United
Nations resolution denouncing the invasion. The three Western forces
retreated, Nassar declared a great victory and the British, only recently
the world's most dominant military power, closed down all its military
bases east of Suez. "Over to you!" read a cryptic White House-bound
telegraph from Harold Macmillan, the new British prime minister who
had replaced the humiliated Anthony Eden.

Two months later, the Soviet satellite nation of Hungary made a
brave bid to free itself from Moscow. For a few brief days, it appeared
the Russians would not intervene. Again, the West was fooled. Nikita
Khruschev sent in the tanks, and the rebellion was crushed. *NR* marked
the occasion with a particularly passionate editorial denouncing
Eisenhower for abandoning not only America's historic Western European allies, but also its "Christian allies" in Eastern Europe, while all
the time appeasing the "pagan" Third World masses. Eisenhower had
based his opposition to Suez on the assumption that siding with the
British would alienate America in the emerging nations of Africa and
Asia. *National Review* editors were divided on the Hungarian crisis.
James Burnham called for talks that would result in a united, "neutral"
Germany as a panacea for the entire Eastern Europe problem. Other
editors, especially Willie Schlamm, blasted the idea as yet another form
of Western appeasement.[7]

The Buckleyites' domestic agenda contained the usual broadsides
against the welfare state, and high taxation. The shift toward free trade
marked a major break with some elements of the Old Right. Friederich
Hayek, Henry Hazlitt, Ludwig von Mises, and other masters of the
"Austrian school" that championed free markets were much admired
by Cold War conservatives. In the 1940s and 1950s, free trade remained
a cornerstone of the Democratic Party. An idealistic Tennessean, Cordell
Hull, became the first prophet of global free trade. As a young man,
Hull, who was destined for stardom in the Democratic Party, wondered

why American trade policy (then defined by GOP-style protectionism) only took American interests to heart. Why not a trade policy that benefited all of the world's peoples? Such messianic thinking captured the imagination of Woodrow Wilson, America's first truly internationalist president. Meanwhile, Hull continued to rise in the ranks of the Democratic Party. By 1944, with America at its zenith of world power, Hull was at the controls of the nation's trade policy. There, he carried out an ambitious program that resulted in the first trade deal in which all the world's nations would lower existing barriers and tariffs.[8]

Trade also became a form of foreign policy. Free trade would bring global prosperity; such prosperity was the road to world peace. Without free trade, America's allies might flounder economically. If the latter occurred, those same nations might turn to socialism, Marxism, even alliances with the Soviet Union. Unilateral trade agreements, the thinking went, helped to keep the world safe from Soviet communism. As numerous American industries, including the once-mighty steel, suffered from free trade deals, various Congresses passed protectionist legislation during the 1950s and 1960s. But all immediate post-World War II presidents—Truman, Eisenhower, Kennedy, and Johnson—were free traders and such legislation went nowhere.[9]

The Buckleyites, also under the tutelage of Milton Friedman, swore the same fidelity to free trade. It wasn't a difficult road to travel. There was the influence of Hayek and von Mises, but also the young Buckley himself. Although he would later express some doubts about a free trade ideology, the idea of free markets always coincided with the overall struggle against totalitarianism. Buckley's 1951 book, *God and Man at Yale* quickly became famous for its scouring of the liberal Yale curriculum. Buckley also sang the praises of a laissez-faire economy. Published when Buckley was only twenty-five, *GAMAY* (as *NR* staffers affectionately referred to it) pretty much served as an early manifesto for *National Review*-style conservatism. The dominant protectionist wing of the Republican Party would be challenged and eventually defeated.

The postwar right also fought the culture wars of the 1950s and 1960s. *NR's* social conservatism was strongly influenced by its fidelity to traditional Catholicism. The Buckley's were born into the Church of Rome; other *NR* contributors, such as Kirk and Frank Meyer, became converts. *NR* placed great faith in the Catholic Church as a vital, if not decisive, moral force in the world. Not just anticommunism, but the church's ancient characteristics—the Latin mass, stained-glass windows, male priests, and meatless Fridays, to name a few—all represented a sure foundation in a world driven by the forces of mass and speed. Hence, the dreaded changes brought about by Vatican II, including the doing away of the Latin mass, served as unnecessary and unproductive "reforms" by an institution not meant to be "relevant" to changing times. Traditionalists such as Buckley and Pat Buchanan have both never stopped mourning the old church or pointing out the follies wrought by Vatican II.[10]

The culture wars also included the equally notorious Warren Revolution on the high court. Most controversial was *NR's* opposition to the *Brown vs. Board of Education* ruling on school desegregation in the South. The magazine made both constitutional and cultural objections to the second reconstruction now being rained down on unsuspecting Southerners. Such delicate matters, the Buckleyites believed, were better left to local communities than unelected judges in far-off places. Correcting any injustices should not entail tearing down the entire Constitution. As Thomas Sowell later maintained, American blacks had made steady economic and social progress throughout the decades without the benefit of far-reaching federal legislation. Equality under the law was all any society should strive for. The venerable Agrarian, Donald Davidson, contributed an *NR* essay that enunciated the tenth amendment defense against a court-ordered takeover of the South's public school system. James Kilpatrick, editor of the conservative *Richmond News-Leader*, soon published the even more ambitious *The Sovereign States*. There, Kilpatrick convincingly argued that the states, as Ronald Reagan later contended, made the union; hence, their sovereignty was being severely violated by the court. Showing his usual foresight, Richard Weaver got to the heart of the crisis: such decisions represented a bid by the courts to regulate every facet of American life, including capitalism, private property, individuality, and the family itself. Weaver also made the cultural argument, angrily declaring in *Visions of Order* that "the attempt to 'integrate' culturally distinct elements by court action...[originates] in ignorance, if not a suicidal determination to write an end to the heritage of Western culture." He knew that the multiculturalists were around the bend. Such an opposition was both learned and sober. It was also too late. Roosevelt and Truman's Supreme Court nominees, plus those made by Eisenhower (it was the "Republican" Ike who appointed radical liberals Earl Warren and William Brennan) had done their damage. Eisenhower had no idea Warren would be so liberal; in addition, he long regretted the Brennan appointment. Again, it was too late. No appointees made by a string of Republican presidents, including Ronald Reagan, would dare reverse major decisions made by the Warren Court.[11]

Culture wars aside, foreign affairs really animated and solidified the postwar right. When push came to shove, laissez-faire economics would take a back seat to fighting communism. Writing three years before the founding of *National Review*, the young Buckley admitted that a military empire abroad would mean an eventual acceptance of a welfare state at home. The right, Buckley readily acknowledged, would have to "acquiesce" in big government in order to defeat Soviet communism. A powerful domestic state in the U.S. was preferable to Soviet world domination.[12]

The right's Cold War prophets were Whittaker Chambers and James Burnham. Chambers's autobiography, *Witness*, an account of his life as a young communist, helped to crystallize the struggle in religious terms. Burnham represented a more practical force. His anticommunism went well beyond the containment policy drawn up by State Department bureaucrats. Rather, Burnham and *National Review* aggressively advocated a rollback of the Soviet Empire. Burnham supported the construction of U.S. military bases abroad; he also hoped to set up a university to train young Eastern European émigrés for the new struggle for the world. No fan of abstractions, Burnham urged an appeal to the "historical nationalism" and deep-rooted cultures of captive states, rather than paeans to democracy or capitalism. Rollback gave Buckleyite conservatism a particularly sharp edge. It also allowed them to be effective critics of coming détente policies, ensuring that a wing of the Republican Party would not just hope to contain Soviet communism, but defeat it completely.[13]

Still, a libertarian streak ran strong on the postwar right, especially in the politics and personage of Barry Goldwater. In the late 1940s and early 1950s, there was strong opposition from libertarians to the right's anticommunist crusade. Like Taft, they feared it would become simply a pretext for an American empire abroad, resulting in continuing statism at home—a charge that Buckley had flatly conceded. Russell Kirk opposed both conscription and remobilization. Frank Chodorov and Murray Rothbard dismissed the Soviet threat and saw Moscow's Eastern European conquests as a source of weakness, not as a step toward global empire. Old Rightists such as Flynn, Chodorov, and Rothbard felt that communism would fall under the weight of its own inequity and brutality. Its subjects would eventually rise up and throw off their shackles. Buckley was wrong; Soviet communism was not worth the continuance of big government at home.[14]

Goldwater, however temporarily, united libertarians, traditionalists, and anticommunists. A son of the frontier West, Goldwater, like many Westerners of the old school, harbored a great resentment towards an East Coast ruling class, especially the big banks. In the Old Right tradition, Goldwater also carried a permanent grudge against the New Deal. Echoing the Old Right argument, Goldwater all throughout his career insisted that World War II-era military spending—and not New Deal domestic programs—pulled the nation out of the Depression. Anticommunism was part of the Goldwater agenda, but perhaps only secondary to economics. Critics have long claimed that the Arizonian worried more about union bosses such as Walter Reuther than whatever Nikita Khrushchev was doing in the 1950s.

The right took to Goldwater early on. His 1960 speech at the Republican Party national convention, exhorting conservatives to "grow up" and take control of the GOP inspired a massive draft Goldwater grassroots effort that had the senator's tactical support. Demographics also worked in Goldwater's favor. The media's 1964 front runner, New York governor, Nelson Rockefeller, represented the GOP's losing past: liberal, big spender, a candidate from the urban Northeast. Goldwater symbolized its Sunbelt future: entrepreneurial, anticommunist, with a dash of "traditional values" thrown in. In 1964, abortion and school prayer, not to mention affirmative action and immigration, were nowhere to be seen on the political radar screen. A "religious right" had not yet been born. Social issues revolved around voting and civil rights legislation. Goldwater opposed the 1964 federal civil rights bill, mostly out of private property concerns. Still, it was a vote that Senate Minority Leader Everett Dirksen, himself no Goldwaterite, called one of the most courageous he had seen in his long senatorial career.

After President John F. Kennedy's assassination in November 1963, Goldwater lost what desire he had to run for the presidency. However, the draft Goldwater movement was now far too strong for the Arizonian to back out. Plus, the movement's success had to impress the senator. Perhaps the Sunbelt boys really could take the party back from an East Coast elite.

Conservative intellectuals played a role in Goldwater's rise. Both Russell Kirk and Milton Friedman advised Goldwater and even helped to draft speeches. *National Review* publisher William Rusher was central in organizing the draft Goldwater movement. Buckley, however, was not so enthusiastic. He considered publishing an *NR* editorial urging Goldwater to drop out of the race if he lost the California primary. To carry on after such a defeat would only embarrass the conservative cause. Rusher himself was preparing to resign from *NR* if such an editorial came to pass. But Goldwater defeated Nelson Rockefeller by a slim margin in California, sealing his nomination victory.[15]

What small chance Goldwater had of defeating Lyndon Johnson went up in smoke when the senator, while accepting the GOP presidential nomination, fired back at his tormentors in both the Republican Party and the liberal media. There, Goldwater famously maintained that "moderation in the defense of liberty is no virtue, extremism in the defense of freedom is no vice."

By assailing "moderation," Goldwater was attacking those liberal Republicans dubbed "moderate" by their defenders in the media. Moreover, Goldwater's defense of "extremism" signaled to the media that the John Birchers and the Buckleyites (the latter considered extremists even by Richard Nixon) weren't such bad guys after all. To hell with winning the election. Goldwater's address was, in part, payback time to his enemies.

Although Goldwater had sympathy for Old Right positions, his rise illustrated the gap between his politics and those of Robert Taft. The new conservativism had an expansive worldview, one that preached both global free trade and supported an American military empire all over the world. Taft's America, on the other hand, was generally rural and small town, defined by small businesses with a Main Street rather than a globalist perspective. His vision of the American republic was both more backward looking and remarkably modest. On trade and foreign policy, Taft tended toward an America First stand. He cared more, for instance, about the survival of the shoemaking industry in America than whether American consumers could someday buy $125 sneakers made by twenty-five cents an hour labor in Indonesia. His non-interventionism did not mean disarmament. However, Taft had no desire to spread American-style secular democracy to all parts of the earth. An aggressive perusal of American Empire would only earn the country many bitter and lasting enemies throughout the world.

Besides his lingering opposition to the New Deal, Goldwater's campaign collided with other values held by an emerging suburban America. The new middle class despised tax increases, but also demanded a welfare state in the form of Social Security, Medicare, spending for public schools, and college loan programs. This also is where Goldwater tripped up badly. His intelligent arguments against Social Security and boondoggles such as the Tennessee Valley Authority, both straight out of the conservative tradition, helped to sink his campaign. By the 1960s, Americans were content with the New Deal. Whatever opportunities to dismantle that regime in the 1950s were ruined by both the Cold War and a passive Eisenhower administration. However, conservatives would learn from Goldwater's mistakes. The protectionist wing of the GOP also faded away under the case for consumer "choices." Free trade gave Americans more goods to choose from. Such competition lowered prices, too. The idea of Americans as mere consumers began to drive the free trade argument. The suburban shopping mall and superstores such as Wal Mart quickly threatened to make both Main Street and their Mom and Pop country stores obsolete. Economic growth became almost a do or die proposition for the country. Economics and economics alone, seemed to define the nation's destiny. The best attempts by traditionalists aside, the country had entered the post-Christian age.

Still, the decade from 1955-1964 were *National Review's* golden years. The *NR* of the 1950s and 1960s never lost its ability to amuse and provoke. A week after Lyndon Johnson became president, the publication, for instance, ran a one-sentence editorial declaring that their "patience with the Johnson administration had been exhausted." With his syndicated column and television talk show, Buckley served as a model for future conservative pundits, including George F. Will, Patrick Buchanan, and James J. Kilpatrick, to name just three.

In 1965, Buckley ran for mayor of New York City. Hot button issues such as welfare spending and school busing dominated a campaign that presented Buckley as the conservative alternative to John Lindsay, the Republican nominee who proudly accepted the endorsement of the state's Liberal Party. Lindsay was also being groomed as a future presidential candidate, an East Coast liberal who might take the party back from Goldwaterite "extremism." Buckley lost, but his candidacy represented a serious attempt to keep Goldwater-style conservatism alive. The sharp-witted commentator also made hash of his rival's wooden campaigning style, thus drilling holes into any notion of Lindsay being presidential material. The next year, Ronald Reagan was elected governor of California. In Reagan, conservatives would find the ultimate hero: witty and genial where Goldwater was candid and gruff, Reagan presented a nonthreatening, optimistic, "smiling face" to American conservatism.

Nonetheless, most conservatives preferred Richard Nixon over Reagan at the 1968 GOP convention in Miami Beach. Buckley, for one, felt Reagan lacked an intellectual brain trust apparently necessary for any successful administration. "Where are the Sorensons?" he quipped to an eager young Reaganite making the case for his candidate in Miami. In 1960, there was no endorsement for Nixon from *National Review*. By 1968, the same Nixon was acceptable to a movement badly battered by their 1964 shellacking.

As a result, the 1970s were a time of disappointment for the Buckleyites. Their rebellion against the Nixon administration only produced John Ashbrook's maverick candidacy, which garnered just 10 percent of the vote in the 1972 New Hampshire primary. Following Watergate and the fall of Nixon, Rusher and New Right leader Richard Viguerie made a serious attempt to form or support a third-party challenge to the GOP. Rusher hoped to enlist his friend Ronald Reagan in the cause. However, Reagan, then retiring as California's chief executive, stayed put in the GOP, choosing to challenge President Gerald Ford in the 1976 primaries.

Overall, political and social trends in the country continued to turn against the right. The 1970s were a decade of détente with the Soviet Union. Although supported by the public, conservatives, especially Buckley and Rusher, denounced Nixon's opening to Communist China. They were bitter critics of détente and as such, prophets of a coming "second Cold War" that dominated American politics in the 1980s. Indeed, following America's defeat in Vietnam, the Soviet Empire advanced into several Third World countries, including Nicaragua, a nation in the heart of Central America.

The cultural scene was similarly dismal. Nixon's attempts to place Southern conservatives on the Supreme Court (first Clement Haynesworth, then Harold Carswell), were shot down by a liberal-dominated Senate. Instead, Nixon settled for "moderates" such as Lewis Powell and Harry Blackmun, both of whom helped to advance the Warren Revolution. Blackmun, for instance, wrote the 1973 Supreme Court decision *Roe vs. Wade*, which gratuitously took the abortion issue out of the hands of state legislators, making nearly all forms of that procedure legal. Other Supreme Court decisions enshrined divisive affirmative action programs. In addition, school busing rulings in Boston and New York City brought the desegregation crisis up North. Local communities in these entities, like their counterparts down South, saw control of their public schools disappear. Massive middle-class flight from the cities to the suburbs continued, further stratifying the nation along lines of race and class. The economy, meanwhile, suffered from shocks caused by de-industrialization and occasional high inflation and rising interest rates.

In 1978, Buckley gave a speech at the University of Notre Dame. There he echoed Alexander Solzhenitsyn's earlier, similarly gloomy prophecy for a West wallowing in cultural decadence. "It is idle to talk about preventing the wreck of Western civilization," Buckley remarked, quoting his old friend Whittaker Chambers, "it is already a wreck from within."[16]

Old Rightists would have some sympathy for such remarks. Gloominess aside, the right would be replenished by two strains of conservatism, different in temperament, but both claiming to revitalize a movement demoralized by the Nixon years.

The New Right, which flourished in the late 1970s, had its roots firmly in the Goldwater movement. Richard Viguerie, Phyllis Schafly, Howard Phillips, and Paul Weyrich all supported Goldwater in 1964 and were generally receptive to *National Review*-style conservatism. However, the New Right presented itself solely as a Middle America movement, populist in nature, and scornful of an East Coast elite that Buckley, beginning in the 1970s, often socialized with. Although sufficiently anticommunist and opponents of "big government" (and big business), the New Right jumped headfirst into the social issues of the day: Abortion, school prayer, busing, pornography, and the establishment of religious schools to combat the continued secularization of public education.

The New Right coalesced around Viguerie's *Conservative Digest*, a monthly that was patterned after *National Review*, with the cartoon spread in the middle and the Viguerie columns in the back. Direct mail, attack ads, criticism of the GOP as an incurable set of country clubbers in dire need of populist foot soldiers also characterized these brash conservatives. Paul Gottfried, an otherwise sympathetic observer, noted some intellectual deficiencies in this movement. The New Right knew what they were against. However, what were they for? "It is all very well to talk of traditions and values, but problems arose over the details," Gottfried noted. "Are Rousseau and Hume, both skeptics, part of the preferred tradition? What of the pagan classics that many Evangelical Christians object to?" The New Right, he added elsewhere, would not receive widespread favorable attention "until their values are shared by prestigious universities and leading novelists." That was never a possibility. New Right literature made little mention, if at all, of Kirk, Weaver, Burnham, Kendall, Nisbet, or other important conservative thinkers.[17]

With not only Ronald Reagan's election, but also the triumph of a Republican-controlled U.S. Senate, the New Right claimed victory in 1980. As Howard Phillips later pointed out, many Republicans elected to the Senate ran ahead of Reagan in their state's popular vote. Reagan, Phillips maintained, rode on their coattails, not the other way around. Winning elections was the easy part. Once the New Right marched with Reagan into Washington, the problems began.

The New Right was quickly seduced by the capital city. They wanted their people at the controls of the bureaucracy, where presumably they would either eliminate or drastically scale back the federal leviathan. Such appointments, however, could never happen. Whenever Reagan deviated from his conservative beliefs, Viguerie and others bitterly blamed James A. Baker III, Reagan's chief of staff and former George Bush campaign manager, for the Gipper's heresies. It was never Reagan's fault, only the people around him.

Throughout the 1980s, the New Right remained outsiders in Reagan's Washington. It was easy to see why. First, New Right leaders never endorsed Ronald Reagan in the 1980 primaries, giving support to John Connally or Phil Crane, instead. Moreover, the 1980 *Conservative Digest* endorsement of Reagan "did not extend" to running mate George Bush. Secondly, the Reaganites wanted no part of the New Right's social agenda, especially busing, abortion, and affirmative action. Mailing lists aside, New Right leaders did not build up and solidify a militant, Middle America-based movement. Perhaps, they lacked the resources and numbers to do so. Instead, they tried playing power politics with a GOP establishment that wouldn't even give these boys a few crumbs from the table. In 1983, Viguerie again toyed with the idea of starting a third party. That was not doable, but as with Pat Buchanan, a third party was Viguerie's natural home. In 1991, this is where Howard Phillips ended up, creating his U.S. Taxpayers' Party, later renamed the Constitution Party. By then, Viguerie, after some failed business ventures and an unsuccessful 1985 run in Virginia's lieutenant governor's race, was forced to sell *Conservative Digest*, which itself would eventually go out of business.

As opposed to the New Right, the neoconservatives would pride themselves on a literary and intellectual style. An example was the

Public Interest, a journal founded in 1965 by Irving Kristol, Nathan Glazer, and Daniel Bell. All three were anticommunist, welfare-state liberals dismayed by the "frothy ideological climate" brought on by Great Society spending programs. In the 1950s, Kristol, a former assistant editor at *Commentary*, was now editor of *Encounter*, an anticommunist journal that attracted many brilliant thinkers from both sides of the Atlantic. In the mid-1960s, *Commentary,* then edited by Norman Podhoretz, remained on the anticommunist left, but the *Public Interest* would begin the march to the right. Podhoretz and *Commentary* soon followed. The *Public Interest* also caught the eye of Robert L. Bartley, Jr., the young editorial-page editor of the *Wall Street Journal.* By the early 1970s, Kristol would be named to the paper's board of contributors, thus giving him a platform to write an occasional column that would reach a mass audience.[18]

As much as William Buckley shaped conservatism in the 1950s, Kristol, an New York intellectual influenced in part by fellow Cold War liberal Sidney Hook, was the driving force behind an ascendant neoconservativism. In addition to editing the *Public Interest*, Kristol issued a catchy description of the breed, "a liberal mugged by reality." This statement reflected the fact that most leading neoconservatives were urbanites, natives of large cities, in particular, New York. The latter fact also served to explain the very large publicity they received. Here were New Yorkers (Kristol, Podhoretz), both longtime liberals, now in alliance with the Buckleyites. For the New York intelligentsia, this was the ultimate act of heresy.

In many respects, Kristol was the most conservative of the neos. He had little problem with the social agenda of the Moral Majority, including the school prayer issue. In the mid-1980s, he counseled his fellow Northeasterners not to worry about a new populism brewing in the heartland. It was only a revolt by decent, traditionalist-minded folk. Earlier, in the 1950s, the young Kristol held some sympathy for the embattled Senator Joe McCarthy. While not endorsing the man, Kristol knew that McCarthy's popularity was due to the latter's scathing critique of a ruling class that had helped to sell out much of Europe and Asia to the communist giants. Pat Buchanan and other Old Rightists made similar analyses.

Still, Kristol was no Buckleyite ready to carry a banner first raised in the 1950s. Although *Encounter* was anticommunist, Kristol considered American conservatives far less intelligent than their British counterparts, nearly all of whom accepted the welfare state. In the 1950s, he told Clinton Rossiter that the American right was too backward and reactionary, too given to "crackpotty" ideas. Even after coming over to the right, Kristol never fully abandoned those earlier views. He recalled that while his friends had no use for Great Society social engineering, *National Review*, even in the mid-1960s, was "too right wing" for their tastes. In addition, the Republican Party itself was far too enthralled by big business and budget-balancing to care about the ideas of intellectuals. In time, however, the GOP became more hospitable to Kristol and his colleagues. By the mid-1990s, with the GOP in control of Congress, Kristol was pleased with the progress the party had made. He pointed to a change in rhetoric, most notably the time when Ronald Reagan, while accepting the 1980 GOP presidential nomination, praised the legacy of Franklin Roosevelt, or when Newt Gingrich, after becoming speaker of the house, declared FDR to be "the greatest president of the twentieth century." Conservatives had come a long way from the not-too-distant past when FDR's New Deal represented the devil, Socialism, Inc., in the once-free USA.[19]

The Buckleyites' strong internationalism made it easier for these newly minted neoconservatives to make a final break with the left. But it was the crushing defeat suffered by Barry Goldwater in 1964 that gave them a golden opportunity to change the direction of American conservatism. They championed a pro-democracy foreign policy, rather than one that viewed the Cold War as a titanic culture war. Toward that end, the neos supported the creation of a new federal bureaucracy to spread the virtues of democracy to even those nondemocratic nations that posed no threat to the United States. Similarly, tax cuts, not frontal assaults on New Deal and Great Society-era spending programs, informed a new fiscal policy. Neoconservatives opposed quotas, welfare state excesses, and school busing. On the latter issue, they again took a different track: instead of making constitutional arguments, school busing, they argued, was a failure because it did not, as advertised, help inner-city blacks achieve greater academic achievements.[20]

On all issues, foreign and domestic, neoconservatives were far more articulate and successful than their New Right counterparts. The supply side idea appealed to conservatives still haunted by memories of 1964. Rather than be accused of a stingy, "Hoover-like" obsession with balanced budgets and spending cuts, the GOP could now present an optimistic, upbeat program to the nation. In the tradition of JFK, tax cuts and deregulation would get the country moving again.

That the neoconservatives had a sympathetic hearing at both the *Wall Street Journal* and the *New York Times* didn't hurt, either. By 1980, the *Journal's* editorial page, which preached free markets, tax cuts, and open immigration, had now supplanted *National Review* as the most influential voice on the right. Since neoconservatives did not promise to lead an angry populist revolt from Middle America, the media could not lampoon them as right-wing ideologues. And so, the 1980s saw the maturation of the famous conservative tripod: less spending and lower taxes for the economy; a foreign policy promoting a strong defense, anticommunism, and now, a crusade for global democracy; and "traditional values" (the family, marriage) on the social issues front.

The 1980s also saw some criticism of the Reagan administration from the establishment right. There was unhappiness over Reagan's 1982 tax increase, his ending of economic sanctions against Poland's communist regime, and his affirmative action choice of Sandra Day O'Connor as a Supreme Court justice. After the 1982 tax increase, Viguerie published an issue of *Conservative Digest* solely dedicated to highlighting the administration's many failures. Page after page ripped the Reaganites on a number of issues: deficit spending, détente with the Soviets, illegal immigration. Still, that publication would endorse Reagan's reelection bid in 1984, namely out of opposition to Walter Mondale.

Criticism of the administration remained muted throughout much of Reagan's second term. Typically enough, the biggest disagreements came over foreign policy. Reagan's détente with Mikhail Gorbachev was bitterly denounced as appeasement by a number of increasingly disgruntled conservative pundits. In 1988, the U.S. Senate easily approved the IMF arms control agreement, which removed both U.S. and Soviet intermediate missiles from European soil. That same summer, Reagan stood in Moscow's Red Square claiming that talk of the Soviet Union as an "evil empire" was all in the past, relics of "another time, another place." Meanwhile, angry New Rightists slammed Reagan as one of those "useful idiots" that Lenin hoped was abundant among the Western political and business elite.

The end of the Cold War in 1989 proved that Reagan's mellowing was warranted. The hawks could make their own claims. The Reagan Doctrine of arming anticommunist guerilla insurgencies successfully harassed the Soviet Empire on the margins in the third world. Gorbachev's maneuvering to seek Western aid and his slightly liberalizing policies of *perestroika* and *glasnost* made any Brezhnev-style crackdown on Eastern European subjects impossible. Reagan was right to seek out and encourage Gorbachev. The Soviet leader, in turn, did not use force to keep the old empire together. The nations of Eastern Europe were allowed to leave the Warsaw Pact in peace. This turn in foreign affairs, plus steady domestic economic growth, convinced conservatives that the 1980s had been their "golden age," an "heroic age," a Garden of Eden they must someday find their way back to. By winning the Cold War, Reagan had done his duty. His presidency was an unqualified success. With that struggle over, it was time to confront the nation's mounting social and cultural ills.

4

The Chapel Hill Conspiracy

Even so, some uneasiness set in once the Berlin Wall fell and the great crusade ended. In February 1990, William F. Buckley, Jr. published a much-discussed *National Review* cover story, simply entitled "What Now?" The essay touched on familiar themes: trade, taxes, abortion, the environment, euthanasia, urban problems, and drugs. Buckley supported an interventionist, generally pro-human rights foreign policy. He also endorsed the idea of voluntary "national service" as a way to maintain a "sense of community" in a time when "high and illegal immigration and...factionalism...encourage centrifugal forces in our culture." Around this time, Buckley had also published a book, *Gratitude: What We Owe Our Country*, where he first introduced his national service idea. The volume was reviewed on page one of both the *New York Times* and *Washington Post* book review sections. Editors at *NR* considered this a sign of success, only to be rebuked by Milton Friedman, who claimed that national service schemes served the centralizing cause of the left, hence the critical attention being paid by the nation's two most important liberal newspapers over a book by America's leading conservative pundit.[1]

Prior to the publication of "What Now?" Buckley presented his ideas to a "conservative summit" held at the Union League in New York City. Norman Podhoretz and Irving Kristol represented the neoconservatives, while Paul Weyrich showed up as a remnant of the New Right. One element of the movement not invited to the summit were representatives of the Old Right. "I suspect these people weren't there because they have made a career out of attacking so many people who were there," Weyrich told a *Washington Times* reporter. *Chronicles*, the flagship publication of the Old Right, published by the Rockford Institute in Rockford, Illinois, had earlier made waves by calling for restrictions on immigration into the United States. A review essay by *Chronicles* editor Thomas Fleming in *NR* criticizing the Lincoln legacy was also a recent bone of contention as was a *Chronicles* essay by Bill Kauffman praising longtime Buckley and Podhoretz nemesis, Gore Vidal.[2]

Being banned from the summit hardly bothered the editors at *Chronicles*. Out in Rockford, no one wondered what came next. Open to the opinions of such writers as Murray Rothbard, who had long opposed both the New Deal and Cold War-style conservatism, the paleos were more than willing to take contrary positions on all issues, foreign and domestic. The think tank with a modest budget would formulate a worldview that rocked the seemingly impregnable conservative movement, spinning the right into some of its worst infighting of the entire post-World War II era.

Important political movements in American history are often inspired or abetted by modest-circulation journals of opinion, which in turn are expected to address controversial issues and take stands in a far bolder style than anything daily newspapers or middlebrow weeklies would imagine. Ideas that originally appear in such a journal hope eventually to find their way into large-circulation publications, gaining exposure to both the masses and their political leaders. Obvious examples are the influence the *New Republic* had on the New Deal and *National Review's* role in shaping the Goldwater movement. Furthermore, since *Time* and *Newsweek* are liberal journals for the masses, they both are often influenced by articles first published in the *New Republic*. A piece that runs in *TNR* on any number of issues may find its ideas repeated in *Time* or the *Washington Post*. From there, it may travel to the even more influential world of broadcast media including the evening news, cable, and radio talk shows.

Such journals need a forceful editor to shape a vision that grabs the attention of the Fourth Estate. The right has seen such editors: Buckley, of course, at *NR*; Norman Podhoretz at *Commentary*; and Kristol at the *Public Interest*. The man who would make conservatives notice Rockford was Thomas Fleming. Fleming's conservatism was strongly rooted in the decentralizing Old South tradition. Fleming was also a trained classicist; the influence of the ancient Greeks and Romans remained central to him. He was also influenced by such Christian apologists as G.K. Chesterton and T.S. Eliot, plus the more unreconstructed Vanderbilt Agrarians. Indeed, the Rockford Institute would inaugurate an annual award in creative writing in Eliot's name and a scholarly letters award

named after for Richard Weaver. Finally, Fleming saw value in the revolt by Western and Midwestern state populists against the welfare-
warfare state of the 1930s and 1940s.

Fleming had roots in both the Midwest and the South. A native of
Wisconsin, Fleming's family would eventually move south to Charleston, South Carolina, where his father owned a minor league baseball
team. Fleming himself was raised in nearby Mount Pleasant. He adopted
the South as his home region, and read extensively in the various fields
of Southern letters. After graduating from the College of Charleston,
Fleming enrolled in the University of North Carolina to pursue a Ph.D.
in the classics. Attending Chapel Hill at the same time were Sam Francis
and Clyde Wilson, both of whom were also pursuing graduate degrees.
Both men would prove to be valuable allies in the many battles years
hence.

In 1989, the Rockford Institute awarded its annual T. S. Eliot Award
for Creative Writing to the novelist Walker Percy. As Fleming introduced Percy to *Chronicles'* other editors, the novelist, himself a Chapel
Hill graduate, joked, "Tom, what kind of magazine are you running? It
looks like a Chapel Hill conspiracy."[3]

That UNC would be the training ground for this movement's thinkers seems out of place, similar to the Agrarians finding root at Vanderbilt.
Following World War I, both Chapel Hill and Vanderbilt advertised
themselves as New South universities, proud of their standing as centers of a "progressive" thought that would leave the old, Jeffersonian
vision behind. It took several decades before the Vanderbilt establishment truly recognized the achievement of the Fugitive-Agrarian-New
Critic movement. In 1980, when English professors at Vanderbilt
planned a grand fiftieth anniversary for the Agrarian manifesto, the
university's president groused over the idea, complaining that his institution ought to be known for other things than such revolutionary texts
as *I'll Take My Stand*. Likewise, Chapel Hill, especially with its Soci-
ology Department had striven, had striven mightily to earn the liberal/
progressive label it would receive from academics outside the region.
Still, administrators at Chapel Hill retained a traditionalist curriculum.
Old Rightists, including its Chapel Hill graduates, would maintain that
the late 1960s, for all their turmoil, represented the last time in America
when young people could receive a truly rigorous, worthwhile education.

After earning his Ph.D., Fleming taught briefly at UNC and then,
even longer, at Miami University in Ohio. In the late 1970s, he re-

turned home to South Carolina to serve as a headmaster at a local private academy. There, he launched a magazine. In 1979, *Southern Partisan Quarterly Review* appeared. To Fleming, such a journal was necessary because the South—the nation's most tradition-filled region, large in size, population, and possible political clout—lacked a journal explicitly Southern in its literary, religious, political, and philosophical worldview. Literary journals such as *Southern Review* and *Sewanee Review* did not, in Fleming's estimation, defend the conservative Southern tradition. The region's hugely popular middlebrow publication, *Southern Living*, got off to a great start in the 1970s, only to be swallowed up by a large Manhattan conglomerate. Such an acquisition would eliminate any conservative views that large-circulation magazine might entertain.

Fleming had ambitious plans for his publication, even hoping that "SPQR" might become a "New Yorker" of the South. For this enterprise, Fleming found a valuable partner in Clyde Wilson, then a history professor up the road at the University of South Carolina. At Columbia, Wilson would eventually edit the papers of John C. Calhoun. Most importantly, he shared Fleming's unreconstructed reading of Southern history. One day in 1978, Fleming drove to Columbia to meet Wilson and plot strategy. There, the two agreed to collaborate on the project.

Two books, both published in the early 1980s, also gave Fleming, Wilson, and Sam Francis (an early columnist at *Southern Partisan*), exposure to critics, if not larger audiences. In 1981, Wilson's book, *Why the South Will Survive*, another event commemorating the fiftieth anniversary of *I'll Take My Stand*, appeared. Wilson, Fleming, Francis and a fourth *Southern Partisan* columnist, John Shelton Reed (who wrote under the pen name of "J. R. Vandover"), were joined by more well-known contributors: M.E. Bradford, Cleanth Brooks, George Garrett, Marion Montgomery, and Andrew Lytle.

By 1980, Lytle, along with Robert Penn Warren and Lyle Lanier, were the three living contributors left from the 1930 classic. But only Lytle, as unreconstructed as ever, contributed to Wilson's volume. As the title suggested, the collection held a guarded optimism; it was also more reflective than polemical. Fleming delivered a paper on the classics and its once-strong influence on Southern education and culture, while Francis, writing at the height of Cold War tensions, criticized an interventionist foreign policy, inspired by a "Puritan Yankee" establishment, one that either fought wars for the sake of people on distant continents or for such abstractions as democracy and progress in the

Third World—but never for direct American interests. Francis called for Southerners to instruct the nation on the "meaning and importance" of a public order and to articulate a foreign policy made for "the protection of the historic character and identity of the community." The essay was both anticommunist and in its own way, America First. *Why The South Will Survive* was especially graced by a stirring call by M.E. Bradford for Southerners to "cultivate the arts of memory" as a way to preserve and strengthen their heritage. Lytle delivered his own moving essay, one that recalled the Old South as a remnant of Christendom, with the region's "republic of families" serving as a steady bulwark against state tyranny.[4]

In 1982, on the heels of Ronald Reagan's landslide presidential victory, Robert Whittaker, another South Carolina traditionalist, published *The New Right Papers*. The collection was a mixture of longtime *National Review* hands (William Rusher, Jeffrey Hart), New Right spokesmen (Paul Weyrich, Richard Viguerie), and writers who would form the heart of an emerging paleoconservatism (Fleming, Wilson, Francis). Populist in its tone, *The New Right Papers* cautiously celebrated the renewed vigor of Richard Nixon's "silent majority," those "Middle America radicals" with the potential strength to wrestle political power away from the Washington elites. Restoration of the nation's republican liberties through a resurgent populism was a major theme of the book.

Several of the contributors waxed optimistic about the right's future. As opposed to Nixon, Ronald Reagan was a tried-and-trusted man of the right. One of their own was now in the White House. Turning away from foreign affairs, Francis's essay, "Message from MARs," called on Middle American radicals to begin a thorough decentralization of nearly all government operations, plus "the dismantling of corporate, educational, labor and media bureaucracies." In contrast to the jeremiads he delivered during the 1990s, Fleming himself allowed for some optimism. In "Old Right and The New Right," he declared the "land, home and church" as the only proper foundations for a healthy society. He also expressed hope that a revived social conservatism would unite Middle Americans, North and South, against the determined socialist and ambivalent capitalist, both of whom, either by social engineering or reckless overdevelopment, threatened to obliterate what was left of society's underpinnings.

On a similar theme, Clyde Wilson called for the New Right to create the "political precondition" (i.e., getting government "off our backs") that would give genuine American communities a chance to reinvigo-rate themselves. Wilson's essay, "Citizens or Subjects?" also contained a concise definition of American-style republicanism. Beginning in the mid-twentieth century, democracy, not republicanism, had come to define the American nation. But democracy itself cannot sustain a people, much less a nation. Instead, a return to a classical republic should be the right's most pressing concern. In a republic, the commu-nity—not the government—is the "basis of all things." As Russell Kirk often noted, individual liberty is only tolerable within the bonds of an ordered community. In such communities, democracy is secondary and generally unimportant. The community itself is "superior" to its rulers. Agreeing with Fleming, Wilson defined any real community as an ex-pression "of that unique synthesis of people, culture and land," one that implied "a degree of homogeneity and stability, of givenness."[5]

Both volumes, despite differences in tone and subject, were hom-ages to Middle American traditionalism. If the South survives, then a strong remnant of Western, Christian civilization would remain alive as well. If there were to be a successful conservative revolution, then it would come from a populist uprising in the heartland. Working for the elimination of hundreds of federal programs is the best any Beltway conservatism can accomplish. A Middle American revolution would see plain folk in the South, the Midwest, and the West take back their communities from the judges and "court politicians" inside the hated Beltway.

Meanwhile, the *Southern Partisan Quarterly Review* had published its first number in the fall of 1979. In the inaugural number, Fleming and Wilson laid out the publication's credo. Its traditionalism, among other things, would be a rebuke to a crass New South materialism:

> There are almost no public voices raised in defense of the South and its traditions...We are in danger of losing our identity, especially by the loss of that sense of neighborhood and kinship, of the old way of doing business only with friends and relatives, of the whole spirit which people used to call Southern hospitality...(We must recapture) the commitment to a way of life and a set of common values that cannot be weighed and measured or bought and sold...It is in the spirit of renewed dedication and a revived sense of the Southern identity that we offer (the *Southern Partisan*).[6]

Most fledgling publications in the United States go under within a year of their first number. Such, too, was the case with *SPQR*. The publication folded after only two issues. At the same time *SPQR* was struggling, another South Carolina-based organization, the Foundation for American Education, was also looking for ways to revive an Old South conservatism. The principles behind FAE were one-time South Carolina state legislator Richard Hines, Charles Hamel, and Richard Quinn, a political consultant who often worked side-by-side on local campaigns with Lee Atwater. At first, the FAE people considered starting up a private university. That venture proved too costly, so the trustees showed interest in launching a journal of opinion. This project proved more doable. A longtime activist in South Carolina politics, Hines was familiar with *Southern Partisan*. Fleming and Wilson sold the mailing list to Hines and his friends, and the publication, beginning in late 1981, was reborn.

For this venture, Quinn served as editor-in-chief with Fleming listed as editor. Early numbers ran essays on John C. Calhoun and Jefferson Davis, plus the "Northern Agrarian" Russell Kirk and the longtime traditionalist icon, T. S. Eliot. In the early 1980s, Cold War politics dominated conservative discourse. *Southern Partisan* was duly anti-communist. But economics, including supply-side theories, did not excite the editors. The emphasis on Old South culture and politics made the publication a breed apart. In politics, the model would be such states' rights agrarians as John Randolph and Thomas Jefferson. For culture, the example of earlier unreconstructed giants, especially the Rev. Robert C. Dabney and Albert Taylor Bledsoe, plus the Agrarians and their disciples would serve as what was best and noble about Southern letters. The simple wisdom of certain country music lyrics, especially those of the ill-fated Hank Williams, was yet another vital element of Southern culture.

As with other conservative publications, *Southern Partisan* was given to those bouts of optimism which characterized the Age of Reagan. Reviewing *The New Right Papers*, Quinn hailed that movement as quite different from what the Buckleyites of the 1950s stood for. That generation, Quinn claimed, would rather be "right" than victorious. The conservatism that emerged in the late 1970s, would, on the other hand, be both philosophically articulate and politically successful. Quinn also praised Fleming, Wilson, and Francis as new voices that represented the future of American conservatism. "They are not household names yet," Quinn noted, "but they will be."[7]

Maybe so, but it wouldn't happen during the Reagan 1980s. Fleming hoped to introduce the immigration issue, with the editors declaring it a phenomenon "beyond Reaganomics," something far more important than mere tax and spending concerns. As it turned out, there was much

New Right-like grumbling about both the GOP Country Club crowd around Ronald Reagan and the betrayal of the Gipper's conservative constituencies. Earlier in *The New Right Papers*, Wilson accurately predicted that the Republican Party, an institution constantly in the thrall of big business and multinational corporations, would have no use for cultural warriors from the heartland.

Early Old Right pessimism was influenced not only by Reagan's policies, but a political defeat inflicted on M.E. Bradford. Old Right forays into politics during the Reagan era were few. But Bradford's desire—and his subsequent rejection—to become chairman of the National Endowment for the Humanities served as the Old Right's bruising introduction to the world of Washington-Manhattan politics, where they were hopelessly outgunned by an increasingly wealthy conservative establishment.

While Bradford, especially at the University of Dallas, found satisfaction as a mere "schoolmaster," his ancestors had been politically inclined. Bradford's father had wanted his son to become involved in politics. A combination of scholarship and political activism would carry on an honored Old South tradition. Bradford supported George Wallace's presidential campaigns in both 1968 and 1972, often giving speeches on behalf of the renegade Alabamian. Bradford was also active in Texas Democratic Party politics, even serving on its State Executive Committee. Finally, in 1976, he switched party lines to endorse Ronald Reagan's challenge to Gerald Ford. Intellectuals with a Southern traditionalist bent are rare enough; rarer still, is one who would embrace any Republican Party candidate.

When Reagan was elected president, Bradford appeared headed for formal nomination and confirmation as NEH chairman. This was all many of Reagan's Southern supporters were asking for. They did not seek to have one of their own as a high-profile cabinet member or a Supreme Court justice. Like all other elements of the Reagan coalition, the Old Right felt they were entitled to some plums. After all, the transformation of a Democratic Solid South into a GOP backwater was one of the most significant political phenomena of the last half of the twentieth century. First, there was Storm Thurmond's 1948 third-party run, which netted several Southern states. This was followed by Barry Goldwater's 1964 candidacy, one that put four Deep South states into the GOP column for the first time in American history. In 1968, the New Deal coalition was broken forever, as Richard Nixon and George Wallace, respectively, carried the entire South, with the exception of

LBJ's Texas, which went for Hubert Humphrey. Nixon carried the South along with the rest of the country in 1972. Watergate temporarily broke the GOP's rise, as the South returned to the Democratic fold with Jimmy Carter. Nineteen-eighty, however, saw the South reject its native son for a former Hollywood actor and governor of California. Ronald Reagan wholeheartedly embraced Nixon's Southern strategy and the promise of a new, GOP-dominated Solid South bode quite well for the Party of Lincoln. Although an academic and not an intellectual celebrity, Bradford had numerous former students around the region willing to follow their mentor into the Republican Party. Bradford's own blessing of the GOP cause played its small role in the region's changing politics. NEH chairmanship would be the Old Right's reward.

On the surface, such a post seemed a very modest prize. A relatively small bureaucracy, the NEH has subsidized much serious scholarship, including the papers of such luminaries as James Polk and John C. Calhoun. Eighteenth- and nineteenth-century America lived at the agency. As a *Southern Partisan* editorial claimed, the NEH "to some extent shapes the direction of scholarly effort in this country." And indeed, much of the establishment right went ballistic over the apparent nominee. The "official" explanation was that Bradford, as a one-time supporter of Wallace and more importantly, a scholarly critic of Lincoln, would prove an embarrassment to the fledgling Reagan administration. Bradford could never be confirmed and his defeat (plus, the reasons behind it) would cause unnecessary amounts of bad publicity for Ronald Reagan, a man with much bigger fish to fry. Here was a conservative Republican administration supporting, in one pundit's term, a "Stephen Douglas Democrat." Hence, the Reaganites could be accurately lambasted as the reactionaries the liberal media long claimed they were. Why have such a fierce Lincoln critic in a *Republican* administration?[8]

The claim of "protecting" Ronald Reagan seems dubious. Bradford had the support of numerous senators and congressmen. Senate approval was likely. William F. Buckley, Jr. and Patrick J. Buchanan both supported Bradford. But the opposition, led by Heritage Foundation president Edwin Feulner and Irving Kristol, used their media contacts, especially *New York Times* executive editor A. M. Rosenthal, to turn the Bradford nomination into a battle royal on the right.

Numerous conservatives worried about losing grant money under the new regime. Bradford's political philosophy, alienated the Beltway Right. Not just antistatism, but a devotion to the Old Republic animated Bradford's scholarship. His reading of American history was so compelling, so deeply grounded in an amazing historical scholarship that it could transform a conservatism now enjoying its greatest political triumph. With Bradford at the NEH, the Old Right would have a small, but firm foothold in the culture wars. "Small-r" republican-style virtues of the pre-industrial, pre-welfare state America would be emphasized. Conservatism would be redefined away from those only wanted modest reforms, such as the establishment of a "conservative welfare state." The importance of Western civilization, especially the influence of the old Romans on the Founding Fathers would dominate a Bradford-led NEH. There would be no room for multiculturalist propaganda, an ideology that would come to bedevil conservatives later in the decade.

With a media campaign against him in full swing, Bradford never made it to a confirmation hearing. Feulner and Kristol's choice, William Bennett, then a research director at the University of North Carolina, received the post. Bradford stayed in Texas and published four collections of essays over the next ten years, including the brilliant *Remembering Who We Are: Reflections of A Southern Conservative*. In addition, the Texan kept to a busy schedule of giving lectures nationwide and writing reviews and essays for scores of publications. Bennett went on to greater fame. He served as Reagan's second-term Secretary of Education and later as drug czar during the Bush administration. His 1994 publication, *The Book of Virtues*, a ghostwritten compilation of wise men sayings throughout the centuries, was a national bestseller. Bennett became an icon for cultural conservatives. Rush Limbaugh, for one, credited Bennett as one of his intellectual mentors. Bennett was also given opportunities to run for president in 1992 and 1996. However, citing fundraising problems, he passed up both campaigns.

Old Right bitterness over the Bradford-Bennett struggle never subsided. While the Beltway Right hailed the 1980s as a golden age, the Old Right continued their own critique of that decade. There was, paleos claimed, no Reagan Revolution. On the campaign trail in 1980, Ronald Reagan had promised to eliminate the hated Department of Education. But upon his election, Reagan appointed Terrell Bell, a liberal Republican, to head that bureaucracy. In 1982, the Reaganites did make a belated effort to eliminate DOE, but congressional foes, including many Republicans, easily shot down that idea.

Also in fairness to Reagan, his administration, under the leadership of budget director David Stockman, tried to enact major Social Security reform, one that included real savings in that sacred cow New Deal program. Again, the Reaganites were plummeted, with the U.S. Senate voting 97-0 to prevent any serious Social Security restructuring. In 1982, however, the Reagan administration and yet another dreaded "bipartisan" congressional committee agreed on a payroll tax hike to keep Social Security solvent.

Old Right thinkers liked Reagan. Fleming praised at least the spirit of an early presidential directive, which recognized the sovereignty of each of the fifty states. But again, rhetoric was not accompanied by any substantial action. Public school systems in both the South and many major American cities remained under federal control. Affirmative action programs also survived this conservative administration. On the spending side, not only were cabinet departments spared the axe, but an entire new bureaucracy, the Department of Veterans Affairs was created.[9]

Much Old Right criticism was based on cultural issues. Fleming and Gottfried criticized the Reaganites "serious failure" to address the nation's mounting immigration crisis. Both were also critical of Reagan's decision to sign into law a national holiday for Martin Luther King, Jr., claiming it was yet another affront to Reagan's conservative Southern constituency. Reagan himself benefited enormously from Southern votes, not just in 1980, but as importantly in 1976, when his surprise victory in the North Carolina primary over Gerald Ford had literally saved the former governor's political career. By the time Reagan signed the King holiday into law, George Washington's birthday as a national holiday had disappeared into something called "President's Day." Furthermore, the King holiday was set for the third Monday in January, which for many years was once celebrated in Southern states as a holiday for Robert E. Lee, whose birthday was January 19. With the continual reworking of the calendar, Washington, Jefferson, and Lee were knocked down that much further, all increasingly subjects of neglect, vilification, and hatred.[10]

As part of the new culture war, symbols and artifacts of Southern culture, including the Confederate battle flag, came under increasing attacks from the usual suspects: leftist organizations and editorialists, multinational corporations, and the Democratic/Republican Party ruling cartel. Here was yet another issue that distinguished the Old Right from Beltway conservatives. Editors at *National Review* and the *American Spectator* were careful to have native-born Southerners write their publication's anti-flag articles. For paleos from all of the nation's regions, the flag was a symbol of courage, honor, sacrifice, duty, constitutional government, the defense of home and family; an expression of a distinct heritage. With its St. Andrew's Cross, it was also a symbol of Christian civilization and Christian liberty, dramatizing the American South's standing as a last remnant of Western Christendom. And that, Fleming claimed, was the major reason corporate elites and the leftist organizations they fund, wanted it banned.[11]

In all, the broader assault on the nation's founding Western heritage was the real story of the 1980s. Late in the decade, student demonstrators at Stanford University and elsewhere, demanded that required courses in the study of Western civilization be done away with. Noting that Stanford's "Western Culture" survey was replaced with something called "Cultures, Ideas and Values," Francis claimed that the new curriculum was "intended as part of the radical reconstruction of the American mind and the extirpation of the philosophical roots of Western predominance." The rise of anti-Western ideologies—not Ronald Reagan's moment in the sun or the fall of the Berlin Wall—defined yet another low, dishonest decade dominated by the left. The Beltway Right quickly professed their own opposition to multiculturalism, but paleos were not impressed. Obviously, the problem was more than Ronald Reagan. Reagan was, after all, an elderly man with few "Reaganites" (Ed Meese and Pat Buchanan being the exceptions) around him in the White House. A "conservative crackup" had indeed occurred during the 1980s. And hence, yet another characteristic of the Old Right was soon born: namely, their withering critique of the seemingly triumphant American conservative movement.[12]

Such criticism, of course, differs greatly from what the left has to say. The Old Right does not blast their Beltway brethren for being cold, cruel budget-trimmers. In fact, the mainstream right had become too soft, too timid, too starstruck, too intimidated by the imperial city to pose much of a threat to the entrenched ruling class. Afraid of being labeled extremist by the media, they sought to curry favor from former enemies. Conservatives, as the New Right hoped, did find work in Reagan's Washington. But they soon lost whatever revolutionary fervor they might have once held. Instead of campaigning to eliminate bureaucracies, many conservative bureaucrats wanted funding increases for their "little empires." The leviathan state rolled on, its growth barely challenged.

Behind it all was a failure of rhetoric. Conservatives, Bradford would admit, had not yet discovered a "new language" to accompany their victories at the polls. Even worse was the rise of ex-liberals who still spoke in the "language of the left." Or as Gertrude Himmelfarb readily acknowledged, most neoconservatives were still proud "children of the New Deal." With the Reagan Revolution a political failure, backsliding continued. The 1980s and 1990s saw the appearance of "progressive conservatism" (Jack Kemp), a "kinder, gentler" conservatism (George Bush), "compassionate conservatism" (George W. Bush), "big government conservatism" (Fred Barnes) and "national greatness conservatism" (David Brooks and William Kristol). All roads lead to political power being ever more concentrated in the right's favorite city. In addition, neoconservatives had convinced their battle-weary brethren that such statists as Franklin Roosevelt, Harry S Truman, John F. Kennedy, Martin Luther King, Jr., and especially, Senator Henry ("Scoop") Jackson, were acceptable conservative icons. They also tried to convince the mainstream right that some good things actually had come out of Washington in the 1950s and 1960s. That, too, wasn't a hard sell. It is easy to understand this new reading of history. The Kennedy and Johnson administrations were enthusiastically interventionist. The Johnson years did see a rapid explosion in domestic government spending. It also saw increases in legal immigration, more free trade deals, the invasion of the Dominican Republic (to force out a Marxist regime there), and a heavy escalation of the war in Vietnam. One couldn't get more globalist than LBJ.[13]

Bradford counseled conservatives to go on the offensive, to give up hope of placating the enemy. A "healthy dose of radicalism" was the cure for 1980s-style malaise. Such a strategy was already in the works. In 1984, Fleming left South Carolina for the Midwest; this time for Rockford to serve as managing editor of *Chronicles*. The institute itself had been founded in 1976 by then-Rockford College President John Howard. Disgusted by the often-violent antics of the New Left—and the cave-ins to their demands by university presidents—Howard launched Rockford as a traditionalist, pro-family think tank. It was on family issues where the institute would first make its mark. Rockford advertised itself as formulating "principles for a free society." Strong families were certainly part of the mix. So were independent businesses and schools, constitutional government, plus an emphasis on the classics. During the early 1980s, Fleming occasionally wrote book reviews for *Chronicles*. When *Chronicles* had an opening for its managing editor position, Fleming, who by now had left *Southern Partisan*, was offered the job. At the time, *Chronicles* was edited by Leopold Tyrmand, a Polish émigré novelist whom Fleming later dubbed as "the Jack Kerouac of Poland" in reference to Tyrmand's affection for jazz and bohemian subjects (and living). Fleming fit in nicely with Rockford's overall philosophy, namely that culture must take precedent over politics. The politics of any nation, Tyrmand fervently believed, merely reflects its dominant culture.[14]

In 1986, fate played another twist on Rockford's fortunes. Tyrmand suddenly died and Fleming succeeded him as editor of *Chronicles*. The Cold War was still on, so the changes were not so apparent. But when that conflict ended, sparks would fly.

5

Suicide of the West—Again

Many of the Old Right's political positions are smack in the conservative mainstream: privatizing Social Security, eliminating numerous cabinet-level positions and hundreds of other federal programs, a pro-life stand on abortion, and opposition to affirmative action and quotas. However, there are significant policy disagreements between these factions, much of it connected to different readings of American history.

Although they may not have planned it that way, the immigration issue put the Old Right back on the map. In many respects, immigration was to the Old Right what anticommunism was to the Buckleyites. Scorned during the Reagan years, paleoconservatives had found an issue that grabbed the undivided attention of the Beltway Right. Such books as Peter Brimelow's *Alien Nation*, Chilton Williamson, Jr.'s *The Immigration Mystique*, plus numerous columns by Francis, Buchanan, Charley Reese, and such an occasional fellow traveler as Don Feder, all presented a most thorough historical critique of this nation-breaking issue.

As noted, Fleming tried to revive the immigration debate during his brief tenure as editor of *Southern Partisan*. He wasn't alone in the struggle. At *National Review*, Chilton Williamson, Jr., then that journal's book page editor, also tried to stir interest in the nation's mounting open border crisis. Williamson, a novelist and the son of a longtime Columbia University history professor, had come to *National Review* in the mid-1970s after a brief stint in the publishing business. During the 1970s, legal immigration into the United States was only about half (four million) as the totals reached in the two succeeding decades. However, beginning in the 1950s, immigration from the Caribbean, mostly Puerto Rico, was transforming New York City, headquarters for *NR*. Like Fleming, Williamson had become interested in the immigration issue long before the tidal wave of the 1980s and 1990s hit shore. As book page editor, Williamson gave space to Fleming, Francis, and M.E. Bradford, all of whom shared Williamson's restrictionist views. But the immigration issue rarely got beyond *NR*'s "Arts and Leisure" section. John McLaughlin often mentioned illegal immigration in his "Letter from Washington" column, but that too was an exception for the publication. Immigration was not a big enough issue to warrant steady editorial opinion and feature story coverage. In 1968, Buckley had defended Enoch Powell, the restrictionist British MP, from left-wing criticism on the subject. Other than that, Buckley, like most conservatives, was silent on the issue. In 1990, a frustrated Williamson would leave *National Review* for the more favorable atmosphere at *Chronicles*.

The Old Right view on immigration was essentially in line with *The Camp of The Saints* scenario, the not-so-futuristic 1973 Jean Raspail novel in which a weak and pusillanimous French government, supported by an equally supine media, academic and church elite, allows a flotilla of one million poor, desperate Indian immigrants to flood that ancient European nation. In the novel, third world immigrants in other European nations, most notably Great Britain, also rise up against the ruling elites. Eventually, a *Wall Street Journal*-style open border policy is mandated for every European nation, including once-independent Switzerland.

No civilization can hope to survive never-ending waves of immigrants from cultures alien to its own. That tidal wave may not, as in the case of *The Camp of The Saints*, happen in one mad rush, but millions of legal and illegal third world immigrants streaming into both America and Western Europe on a steady basis was enough to do the job. "Our survival," claimed Fleming, "depends upon our willingness to look reality in the face. There are limits to elasticity, and these limits are defined...by our historical connections with the rest of Europe and in part by the rate of immigration. High rates of non-European immigration, even if the immigrants come with the best intentions in the world will swamp us." Immigration was a problem, but it was symptomatic of a greater disease: namely, a lack of faith of peoples in Europe and North America in the very rightness of their civilization.[1]

And so, immigration, not the Cold War, was the real phenomenon of the post-World War II era. The problem turned out not to be an East-West conflict, but a North-South one, with people from the poor nations of South America, Asia, and Africa seeking work or just the materialistic pleasures of the advanced, but demographically shrinking Western nations. In 1945, British voters shocked the world by throwing Winston Churchill, out of office and replacing him with Labour Party leader Clement Atlee. On the campaign trail, a nervous Churchill had blasted Labour's economic planning policies as the work of a coming "Gestapo" (Churchill was reading Hayek's *Road to Serfdom*). Such language seemed extreme, especially when describing the unassuming Atlee. Still, the new Labour Party was left wing in a way that no modern Western political party had ever been. After being sworn into office, Labour MP's celebrated by singing the notorious socialist anthem, "The Internationale." Their immigration policy was equally radical.

In 1948, Labour deemed that 800,000,000 former subjects of the British Empire now had an automatic "right of residence" in this small, Northern European island nation. In other words, nearly a billion people, mostly from Asiatic and African nations, could, if they wished, settle in Great Britain the next day. Throughout the 1950s and 1960s, the immigration issue simmered in Britain, with numbers ranging from 50,000 to 100,000 to a 1962 peak of 200,000 people entering the country on an annual basis. In the early 1960s, the Conservative Party passed some immigration reform. However, it wasn't until 1968, when Enoch Powell delivered his explosive "rivers of blood" speech in Birmingham did immigration become a national issue. Both the liberal media and the political class savaged Powell, but public opinion was firmly on the iconoclastic MP's side. Dockworkers rallied outside of Parliament in Powell's support, immigration officers at London's Heathrow Airport signed a petition praising him, and tens of thousands of congratulatory letters streamed into Powell's office from all over Britain.[2]

Powell's speech was candid in a style unknown to American politics. He blasted his own government for enacting a suicidal policy, one akin to "a nation busily engaged in heaping up its own funeral pyre." Furthermore, by opening its gates to the Third World, once-peaceful Great Britain was importing a problem that would lead to the same "tragic and intractable" race problem that in Powell's view, had forever plagued the United States. Powell's own Conservative Party quickly got the message. It rode back into power in 1970 after its new leader, Edward Heath, promised real cuts in immigration numbers. Still, to this day, Great Britain remains under siege from its own illegal immigration problem.[3]

The situation across Western Europe was similarly dismal. Following its bloody civil war in Algeria, France suffered its own immigration crisis arising from both that country and other former colonies throughout the Third World. As punishment for World War II, Germany groaned under the most liberal immigration policy in Europe, one imposed on it by the victorious Allies. Smaller nations such as Belgium, The Netherlands, Sweden, Austria, Switzerland, and Denmark all faced refugee overloads. In the years from 1950 to 2000, Europe had seen more immigration than in its previous 500 years alone.

Enoch Powell was hardly the only opponent of mass immigration. Such intellectuals as Stephen Spender and Eugene Ionesco expressed the same alarm over current open border policies. Anti-immigration third parties sprang up in France, Italy, Austria, Switzerland, and Denmark. As in Great Britain, France and Germany passed legislation severely limiting legal immigration. But was it enough? Post-1945 Western Europe was a tired, dying civilization. Worn out by two world wars and made cynical by the cradle-to-grave welfare state, the continent was marked by low birth rates, and defined by a hedonistic culture that liberated adults from the burdens of marriage and family. For the Old Right, the European future-and with it, western civilization—looked more dismisal than ever.[4]

In America, the immigration issue stood non-existent from the late 1920s into the 1950s. No less a leading neoconservative than Nathan Glazer had declared the 1924 Quota Act to be one of the noblest pieces of legislation in American history. Why? Well, in Glazer's view, the legislation gave the tens of millions of European immigrants and their children a chance to assimilate into American life, to cease being hyphenated Americans, and to grow up in a climate of some calm and stability. Eventually, the era of European immigration became mythologized in American history, represented by such figures as one-time New York Governor and 1928 Democratic Party presidential nominee, Al Smith. St. Patrick's Day and Columbus Day parades were viewed as innocent homages to that era. By the 1950s, the descendants of Ellis Island were leaving the cities, moving to the suburbs or the Sun Belt where, as Jimmy Breslin once described his fellow Irish-Americans, they became just another face in the suburban shopping malls.[5]

Hence, the European immigrant wave created the idea of America as a nation of immigrants. With the cult of immigration in place, the battle over this issue would be joined again. In the two decades following the 1924 Quota Act, Franklin Roosevelt gave lip service to nation of immigrants mythology without tampering with laws already in place. After World War II, and under pressure from the Displaced Persons lobby, Presidents Truman, Eisenhower, and Kennedy arbitrarily increased immigration numbers. But only slightly. In 1952, Congress passed the McCarren-Walter Act designed to "best preserve the sociological and cultural balance in the population of the United States." A lame duck President Truman angrily vetoed the bill, but Congress easily overrode the president's wishes.[6]

For Chilton Williamson, Jr., John F. Kennedy was the main villain in the immigration drama of the 1960s. Kennedy was the driving force behind demands for legislation that would eliminate the national origins mandates. The son of a Boston multimillionaire (and former U.S. ambassador to Great Britain), a prep school and Harvard graduate, a wounded World War II veteran, a U.S. congressman, senator, and finally, the nation's youngest (and first Roman Catholic) elected president, Kennedy, it appears, still harbored a permanent resentment toward an imaginary WASP elite. More specifically, he still seethed over the 1924 immigration restrictions. According to Williamson, knocking out the national origin quota became an obsession for a president who rarely displayed much conviction over any political issue. "For John F. Kennedy," Williamson claims, "immigration reform was a club with which to beat down his own social insecurities as well as the cause for them."[7]

Kennedy's attempt at immigration reform during his ill-fated presidency went nowhere, but his assassination on November 22, 1963 elevated him to martyrdom. As such, legislation he coveted, including immigration, would become a top priority for congressional Democrats. What followed in 1965 was a bizarre non-debate, full of modern America's habit for ambivalence and self-flagellation, plus poorly thought out, guilt-ridden actions. Why should the U.S. government do away with a policy that had full support of the public? Well, as Harry Truman claimed, immigration should be tailored along the lines of "how other nations see us." Other nations—and not the American people— would determine American immigration policy. The administration of Lyndon Johnson and liberal editorialists both agreed with such radical guidelines. How, as President Kennedy had asked earlier, could the United States attack "discrimination" abroad when it practiced such measures concerning immigration? How could the United States preach freedom to, for instance, Asiatic peoples when it denied massive Asian immigration into America? It mattered not that such democratic Asian nations as Japan, Taiwan, South Korea, and India maintain to this day a jealous zero immigration policy.[8]

Plus, as several liberal senators pointed out, there would be no great immigration invasion under the new reforms. With 1960s America already reeling from inner-city rioting in New York and Los Angeles, pro-immigration lawmakers were careful to stress that the new legislation would not open the floodgates to massive third world migrations. It would only make America look good in the eyes of a skeptical global village. Senator Edward Kennedy maintained that reform would not mean "one million immigrants coming into our cities each year," while his brother, the junior senator from New York, added that any reform would mean only 5,000 Asian immigrants into the U.S and no more. There were only a few dissenting voices, mostly from such traditionalist Southern Democrats as Sam Ervin and Strom Thurmond. Both men wondered why a Western nation like the United States, after nearly two hundred years of a fairly successful existence, would even risk altering its Anglo-Saxon core, the very civilization that, America its blessed liberties. However, doing away with the Northern European national origin quota fit in perfectly with the revolutionary tenor of the 1960s. [9]

During hearings on the 1965 immigration bill, Myra C. Hecker, a member of the New Jersey Coalition, itself an offspring of a restrictionist organization first formed in the 1920s pointed out technical flaws in the proposed legislation. Mrs. Hecker claimed the legislation had "non quota provisions that would enable any worldwide quotas to be end run." In addition, unused European quota slots would be given to "countries that would use them," namely third world nations with high birth rates.[10]

Mrs. Hecker's warnings proved prophetic. Furthermore, in both 1976 (to celebrate America's bicentennial?) and 1980, family reunification amendments were tacked on to the 1965 bill. Hence, an immigrant was allowed to bring in not only immediate family members, but grandparents, uncles, cousins, nephews, and other distant relatives. These acts alone significantly fueled immigration numbers. In addition, the illegal immigration problem soon appeared with a vengeance. Mexico's own population had soared from ten million at the turn of the twentieth century to up to 100 million a century later. Here, politicians could now express their opposition to illegal immigration without having to do anything about it. The United States savors good relations with Mexico; allowing illegal (and legal) aliens to work in the U.S. with part of their wages going back home helps, at least according to U.S.

officials, to keep the Mexican economy afloat. There is also the matter of guilt over the Mexican War. Texas, California, and other Southwestern states were once part of Mexico, only to be lost in the conflict of 1846-48. Schoolchildren in Mexico know this. A pusillanimous American regime, typically enough, remains highly sensitive over sealing off the U.S. border to its resentful neighbor. Reform legislation originally called for a little more than 300,000 legal immigrants into the country per year. By the early 1990s, the numbers were more than three times that many. The 1965 bill was threatening to become one of the most catastrophic legislative acts in American history.

While at *Chronicles*, Fleming held his own friendly immigration debate with Leopold Tyrmand. The latter generally favored immigration. Tyrmand believed that there were "two Americas," one founded at Plymouth Rock, the other at Ellis Island. (Fleming would have claimed Jamestown as the site of the real founding.) Disagreements aside, *Chronicles* ran a 1986 essay by Clyde Wilson, gently rebuking the notion of America as a "city upon a hill" (a favorite expression of Ronald Reagan's). John Winthrop's vision, Wilson claimed, was based upon piety and exclusiveness, not the "secularized," "universalist" sentiments that had now won over the conservative mind. That a "city upon a hill" should be used as an excuse for mass immigration was an obscene bowdlerizing of American history.[11]

This was only the first shot. With the March 1989 *Chronicles*, the controversy came to a head. Mark Gerson would call *Chronicles'* "Nation of Immigrants" number "one of the most controversial issues...in the history of American conservative journalism." While making the restrictionist case, Fleming counseled moderation, calling for an open debate and prudent measures before "genuine crazies" took hold of the issue. Fleming also dismissed the idea of "cultural pluralism," claiming it was not "the most attractive legacy we can leave to our children." In the 1950s, such sentiments would be taken for granted by conservatives as a vital truth. But the right had mellowed considerably since then.[12]

Chronicles plowed ahead on the issue. In the late 1980s and early 1990s, it was the only right-of-center journal to take a contrary view of large-scale immigration. Arguments were made on economic, environmental, cultural, and moral grounds.

On the economic front, mass immigration creates a large labor pool, one resulting in high unemployment and shrinking wages. Even in a growth period, such high-immigrant areas as New York City, South Florida, South Texas, and California all had unemployment rates significantly higher than the national average. Industrialists have always preferred cheap immigrant labor. This now meant third world workers willing to work in America for third world wages. While agitating for increases in "skilled worker" immigration slots, T.J. Rogers, head of a software firm in California's Silicone Valley, admitted he had recruiting offices on only twenty-six American college campuses. Research by Donald Huddle, professor of economics at Rice University, found that all immigration into the U.S. results in costs of $70 billion per annum to taxpayers, a number that saw no prospects of shrinking in the years ahead.[13]

There were also environmental concerns and the problem of overcrowding. Could that actually happen in "sea to shining sea" America? Well, consider a population growing from 80 million (at the turn of the twentieth century) to 120 million (by the time of World War II) to 180 million (at the time of immigration reform in 1965) to 270 million by the year 2000 to a projected 400 million by 2050 and finally, to a cool 571 million at the end of the twenty-first century. That means more traffic, more pollution, more schools, jails, commercial and residential development. This argument, however, would find few listeners on the right. Conservatives have always enjoyed making fun of "environmental wackos" and their doomsday forecasts.

Both the economic and environmental arguments, had in fact, inspired what few restrictionist forces existed on the left. While the Sierra Club engaged in an internal debate over mass immigration, another environmental group, the Carrying Capacity, warned of water, land, and even food shortages. No nation has the resources to keep accepting an infinite amount of immigrants forever. Economic populists on the left, primarily at *Dissent*, studied the adverse impact immigration was having on urban workers. Most often affected were inner-city blacks, the most loyal Democratic Party constituency. Unlike the open border right, restrictionist liberals were not guilty of breaking faith with their rank-and-file.

But mostly, paleos opposed immigration on cultural grounds. The phenomenon of a Spanish-speaking culture displacing the Anglo, English-speaking populations in Miami, Los Angeles, and much of New Mexico, South Texas, and the rest of the Southwest was the most dramatic proof that assimilation was not working as planned. Or that it was even being attempted. The title of a *Chronicles* collection on immigration, defending an "American identity" is instructive enough. To the Old Right, America was an extension of Western civilization. It was intended by the Founding Fathers to be an Anglo-Saxon-Celtic nation also influenced by the examples of Athens, Rome, and Jerusalem. Large-scale immigration from non-Western nations would, as Fleming maintained, forever spoil a distinct American civilization.[14]

There was also the matter of the culture wars themselves. Immigration and demographics, not appeals to reason, were driving the debate. America was changing. According to the U.S. Census Bureau, "non-Hispanic whites" were, by the year 2040, set to become a minority group in America. Such projections, plus the demographic realities that had already begun to emerge in the 1980s, gave anti-Western propagandists their hate-filled rationale for rewriting the curriculum, knocking out the classics in favor of unknown writers from the idolized third world. Such demagogues have always been with us. In decades past, they usually were confined to ideological fever swamps in just a handful of publications and college campuses. Up until the 1950s, only a small number of Americans attended college. But a pro-Western curriculum reigned. At many colleges, reading the classics was mandatory. Some universities even stipulated that incoming freshmen applicants translate a page of Latin before being admitted. Higher education was about more than getting a good job. It was designed to link rising generations to the Western tradition and its legacy of ordered liberty. Prior to the 1960s, multiculturalists would have been laughed out of the classroom. All that would change rapidly. Shifting demographics gave them the trump card needed to force their anti-Western agenda on a complacent public.

Why the classics? An emphasis on such texts is central to the Old Right worldview. The literature of antiquity, with its tales of honor, courage, and sacrifice celebrated the moral foundations of Western culture. Athens is where Western civilization was born. Its contributions in mathematics, music, drama, poetry, philosophy, and participatory democracy once went without explanation. The Greeks engaged in an intense study of man, pondering the worth of the individual, the importance of community life, debating what it means to be a free man living in a free society. Rome proceeded on the same theme, with its splendid notion of simple justice; namely, equality under the law. The examples of Athens and Rome laid the foundation for Christianity to take root, first in Europe, then on every continent. For centuries it was considered an absolute imperative that the educated class of every nation study the achievement of Athens and Rome. Such was how Western civilization survived and advanced throughout the ages.

The classics also formed the intellectual backbone of the young American republic. The old Romans, with their emphasis on rule of law and loyalty to family, inspired the Founding Fathers even more than ancient Athens. Not that the Greeks didn't influence American notions of liberty, especially the ideals of private property, firearms ownership, low taxation, a free standing militia, and "a cohesive middle stratum," forerunner to a virtuous middle class. With knowledge of the classics, young Americans might learn where their republic came from, and how it might be invigorated.[15]

The cultural argument, however, would not influence the political class. When it comes to education, politicians only want to bring home the bacon. They don't care what the textbooks have to say about American history. Maybe the political argument might grab the GOP's collective ear. Consider such high-immigrant states as California and Texas. In the 1960s, Ronald Reagan had difficulty winning Mexican-American votes in California, but that was when it was still an overwhelmingly Anglo state. Throughout the 1960s, 1970s, and 1980s, California politics was divided into two regions: the Republican, conservative southern part of the state and the more liberal north. But the victorious GOP (including its leader Ronald Reagan) let down its guard on both legal and illegal immigration. And so, California demographics changed dramatically. When Reagan was first elected governor in 1966, the state was 80 percent Anglo. By the late 1990s, immigration, plus large-scale out-migration of longtime natives, had pushed that number down to less than 50 percent. The days of southern California, especially Orange County, as a hotbed of conservative activity and power, were over. The state's congressional delegation was overwhelmingly Democratic, as were both chambers of the state house, which soon debated making a Mexican holiday, "Cinco de Mayo," a California state holiday as well.

Texas was a different matter. Part Southern, part Southwestern in geography, Texas had an identity, specifically one as a conservative Southern state. Unlike either New York or California, Texas conjures up certain cultural mores and traditions. By the 1990s, Texas was the GOP's most important large state. The party could live with losing California and New York, but not Texas. Immigration was transforming this state, too. In 1968, 12 percent of Texas was Hispanic. By the late 1990s, the number reached 30 percent. To be sure, the political culture in Texas is different than California's. Residents of a state with no income tax and one proud of its pro-gun heritage, Hispanics voted in large numbers for such Republicans as Kay Bailey Hutchinson and Phil Gramm. Hispanic Catholics, especially in the Corpus Christi area, were among the most heavily pro-life activists in the nation. Still, on local, state, and national levels, most Hispanics voted Democratic. The state's congressional delegation, like those in New York and California, was solidly Democratic. A diminishing few Texas Democrats are conservative; most, however, are liberals with voting records the *New York Times* could agree with. Some Texas lawmakers complained about illegal immigration, but only a few about the much-higher legal influxes. What if immigration into Texas continued at present rates? Would it still be in the GOP column or would its politics resemble a Massachusetts in the Southwest?

At its 1998 state convention, rank-and-file Texas Republicans denounced current immigration policies and adopted a resolution calling for a return to pre-1965 standards. However, the state's popular governor, George W. Bush, dismissed that plank and announced he would not run on it in the fall campaign, echoing sentiments his father often made about national Republican Party platforms. Bush Junior, of course, was heir to an investment banking family from Greenwich, Connecticut. Another pro-immigration Texas politician, Dick Armey, was a native of snowy North Dakota. In 1996, Armey, as House Majority Leader, worked hard to defeat legislation calling for modest cuts in legal immigration. These two "outsiders," one a northern transplant, the other, a son of one, clearly favored the immigrant over the Texas native. For liberals, the sweetest victory may be forthcoming in decades hence, when the Nixon, Reagan, and Bush (I and II) administrations are long forgotten. Republicans will continue winning elections. But to what end? The Republican Party congresses of the 1990s refused to abolish affirmative action programs; they also increased funding for bilingual education—and hundreds of other federal programs. Such "revolutionaries" spent tax dollars at a faster rate than the Tip O'Neill-run Democratic congresses of the 1980s. Replacing the old Southern strategy with an "Hispanic strategy" only served to move the GOP even further to the left.[16]

However, the strongest brief against immigration was, ultimately, a moral one. Americans never voted for such a demographic upheaval. In 1965, their lawmakers told them that no demographic change would occur at all. The nation was changing against the will of the public. It mattered nothing that Americans, though opposed to immigration, put up little resistance to a policy they disliked. They still were being betrayed by a cynical, ravenous elite beholden only to pro-immigration cash cows on both Wall Street and in corporate America. Immigration left Americans, as a people, with no control over their demographic destiny.[17]

The Old Right had policy objectives concerning immigration: A moratorium similar to the one enacted in 1924, sealing off America's borders to illegal aliens, and the deportation of illegals already in the U.S. (this would include legal immigrants, such as students and workers who had overstayed their visas). Then, assimilation might work as it had in the past.

Paleos also wanted to start a dialogue and debate among conservatives on this issue. The cultural argument, they hoped, would stir interest among the establishment right, which nominally at least, declared an interest in fighting the culture wars. If the right was as "pro-Western" as it claimed, then opposition to massive non-Western immigration might seem a logical position to take. A united conservative front on immigration would grab the attention of the mass media; from there, it might influence lawmakers, just as the right's old anticommunist stand had an impact on the post-Eisenhower GOP. An anti-immigration argument being made by just one conservative publication (and one well outside the Beltway at that) could hardly have any influence in Washington's arrogant halls of power.

At first, the Rockford Institute was on the receiving end of the usual invective. Fleming's criticism of cultural pluralism did not sit well with the East Coast right. "I know the enemy when I see him," Norman Podhoretz wrote Richard John Neuhaus, "and as far as I'm concerned, *Chronicles* is it." Edwin Feulner agreed, promising that "ICBMs" would be coming Rockford's way if *Chronicles* did not pipe down.[18]

And indeed, the ICBMs did come, namely in the form of lost grant money—such money being mother's milk for any journal of opinion. According to Fleming, Rockford, over the years, "lost millions" once the controversy over immigration broke. *Chronicles'* stand originally gained no new converts. The *Wall Street Journal* remained as extremist as ever on the subject. Up until 1994, it still ran its boastful Fourth of July editorial calling for a "there shall be open borders" constitutional amendment. California's highly popular anti-illegal alien Proposition 187 shot down that annual practice. In addition, the *American Spectator, Commentary,* the *Weekly Standard,* the *Washington Times,* the Heritage Foundation, the American Enterprise Institute, and the libertarian

Cato Institute all continued to oppose deep immigration restrictions. *Human Events*, the East Coast publication with the most populist-leaning readership, was sympathetic to the restrictionists' cause, but that journal hardly made immigration reform a top priority. The most influential conservative during the 1990s was talk show host Rush Limbaugh. A native of small-town Missouri, Limbaugh came to New York City in the late 1980s, where he began his rapid rise to talk show preeminence. Living in a city being overwhelmed by third world immigrants, Limbaugh often fretted on the air over the impact immigration was having on the "character" of the American nation. In 1992, he followed his idol William F. Buckley, Jr. in giving a "tactical" endorsement to Pat Buchanan's presidential campaign. Limbaugh also had nice things to say about the Ross Perot insurgency. However, the Bush administration quickly began wooing Limbaugh, inviting him to the White House and allowing him to spend a night in the Lincoln bedroom. From then on, Limbaugh remained a loyal GOP foot soldier. He also took a conventional stand on immigration: no to illegals, yes to legals. In 1994, this former resident of California supported Proposition 187, but defended his anti-Prop 187 friends, William Bennett and Jack Kemp. Restrictionists found no ally in Limbaugh, either.[19]

In the early 1990s, however, the Old Right found some allies. Pat Buchanan made immigration restrictions part of his 1992 and 1996 presidential campaigns. In the summer of 1992, *National Review* surprised many observers—and incurred the wrath of the *Wall Street Journal*—by publishing a passionate cover story by Peter Brimelow that also severely attacked current immigration policies. The essay, which viewed immigration control as nothing less than a matter of survival for a nation already reeling from mounting social and cultural ills, was later expanded into Brimelow's highly publicized 1995 book, *Alien Nation*, unique also in that it was published by a leading Manhattan firm, in this case, Random House. Under the editorship of John O'Sullivan, a former advisor to Margaret Thatcher, *National Review* devoted scores of editorials, essays, and some cover stories to the issue, most notably a memorable 1994 number scouring the cult of multiculturalism. In addition, the *New York Post* editorial page, under the direction of neoconservative Eric Briendel, also called for immigration reductions. Briendel may have been influenced by his deputy, Scott McConnell, a former *National Interest* editor who was one of the few conservative pundits to praise Buchanan's famous "culture wars" stemwinder at the 1992 Republican Party convention.

This coming of the mind of elements on the right didn't last long. After Buchanan shocked the political world by winning the 1996 New Hampshire GOP presidential primary, he was savaged by the left/right media with a tidal wave of hate-filled rhetoric unseen before in American history. Buchanan's campaign quickly fell apart, while the commentator remained in a Republican Party that had no use for his America First platform. The next year, both O'Sullivan and McConnell lost their jobs. O'Sullivan was fired reportedly because of disagreements over the immigration issue itself at *NR*. McConnell, who became editorial page editor of the *Post* in early 1997, lost his job following a *Post* editorial criticizing the idea of Puerto Rican statehood. Once the editorial appeared, a contingent of New York City politicians of Puerto Rican ancestry, including the Bronx borough president, descended on the *Post's* offices to register their complaints with that newspaper's publisher. McConnell had been in some conflict with the *Post's* hierarchy over other pieces, but this time he was fired, replaced, symbolically enough, by second-generation neoconservative John Podhoretz. The *Post* quietly dropped its restrictionist stance. At *NR*, under new editor Rich Lowry, such a position was significantly muted, no longer the topic for cover stories.

Immigrationists held a few cards of their own. Those who sought to cut off immigration were guilty of the usual charges, "racism" and "nativism," to name only two. There was also the perennial question: Where did *your* ancestors come from? If one's grandparents or great-grandparents were part of the European immigration wave of the late nineteenth and early twentieth centuries, then one had no moral standing to oppose today's almost entirely third world immigration, lest one be guilty of a rank hypocrisy.

For the Old Right, that was not the issue. Instead, it had to do with the 1965 debate on immigration reform when Americans were promised by their leaders that no real change would take place in the nation's population.

The restrictionists' dilemma was very much dialectical. It also mattered nothing that nowhere in the U.S. Constitution is America deemed to be a "nation of immigrants." Nor did it count that the Founding Fathers plainly opposed large-scale immigration and celebrated instead a relatively homogeneous society. The fact that restricting immigration itself is an American tradition was also a non-starter. The "nation of immigrants" cult was now a more sacred cow than New Deal spending programs, more American than the long-lost Constitution or Bill of

Rights. The battle cry "Immigration now, immigration forever!"[20] propagated by the political class and their media allies only made a mere dialogue, much less a resolution on this issue, seemingly impossible to achieve.

6

Against American Empire

During the Cold War years, some paleos were hawks and Reaganites, others weren't. Buchanan and Francis, for instance, both supported the Reagan Doctrine. As director of communications in the Reagan White House, Buchanan even penned some of the strongest pro-Contra rhetoric Reagan would give. But others, especially Bill Kauffman, would join Rothbard (and as such, the spirit of Chodorov and Flynn) in opposing Cold War militarism. Fleming, in fact, later claimed that American involvement in Central America undid the lessons Vietnam taught the budding American Empire. American actions in El Salvador, Nicaragua, and Panama served as predecessors to the post-Cold War hubris the Old Right so energetically opposed.[1]

In fairness to the hawks, Buchanan and Francis were not on a mission for global democracy. They opposed American economic sanctions against anticommunist regimes in El Salvador, Chile, the Philippines, and South Africa. The purpose was to roll back the Soviet Empire, not to force a form of government on other nations. In fact, Buchanan, by 1989, was proposing a grand deal in which the Soviets would pull their troops out of Eastern Europe in return for American withdrawal from Western Europe. "We are not the Romans," Buchanan declared on *Crossfire* the day after the Berlin Wall fell. With the Soviet Empire on the march, American military bases all over the world were a necessary aberration. But with the Cold War over, it was time to reclaim the Old Republic.

Indeed, Cold War hawks and doves were united against the "New World Order" era that emerged with America's 1991 war against Iraq. With Rockford now excommunicated from the establishment right for its stand on immigration, Fleming looked elsewhere for allies. The Ludwig Von Mises Institute in Auburn, Alabama also provided a hospitable atmosphere for dissenting voices. Founded in 1982 by Lew Rockwell, a former aid to the antistatist Congressman Ron Paul, and greatly enhanced by the presence of the libertarian warhorse Murray Rothbard, Von Mises enunciated familiar libertarian themes: free markets, draconian cuts in both the federal budget and taxes of all sorts, and opposition to an interventionist foreign policy. During his two stints in Congress, the indefatigable Rep. Paul refused to vote for any spending measures that were not specifically approved of in the U.S. Constitution. For this, the conservative elite considered Rep. Paul an amusing oddball. Von Mises combined their free market philosophy with a sound traditionalism. Here, a "paleolibertarianism" was born. Not just opposition to quotas and immigration, but also a rousing recognition that Christianity was a good, great force in the world distinguished these libertarians. Rockwell cited both Rothbard and Hayek on the latter subject. For Rothbard, "everything good in Western civilization, from individual liberty to the arts, is due to Christianity," while Hayek claimed that it is to religion that "we owe our morals, and the tradition that has provided not only our civilization but our very lives."[2]

Such talk was rare in libertarian circles. Granted, both Democrats and Republicans give lip service (and nothing else) to conservative Christians, but the Libertarian Party has felt beholden to support among other issues, the legalization of drugs and prostitution, plus unlimited immigration, positions that only offend Middle American sensibilities. True, libertarians do all this in the name of individual freedom, but the movement has never understood the importance of at least the idea of a Christian society to ordinary Americans.

The failure of the Libertarian Party is a shame. Alien positions aside, modern libertarianism represents not only a most brilliant critique of a centralized American regime, but also a pleasing vision of true liberty. Imagine, people living without *all* aspects of the modern state—including a bloated defense budget, not to mention life without income taxes or entitlement programs. The libertarians' broadside against "government" schools is particularly memorable. The state wants to control your children's impressionable minds. The only purpose of government schools is indoctrination. Such unreconstructed Southern apologists as the Rev. Robert L. Dabney couldn't have said it better. Libertarians love to quote from Jefferson, Patrick Henry, George Mason, and other giants of the founding era. And rightly so. Their vision of liberty is often in line with those of the Founding Fathers. The stumbling point, however, remains the question of traditional community life. Or, more specifically, if libertarians even *believe* in such things. As Kirk, Robert Nisbet, and other critics have constantly noted, individual freedom is not enough. Such freedom means nothing without a sense of community.

By the early 1990s, Murray Rothbard had become thoroughly disillusioned with the Libertarian Party's stand on social issues. In the 1970s, the LP did have a window of opportunity to become a force in American politics. President Nixon's "big government conservatism," his wage and price controls, and the general expansion of the welfare state— Nixon even flirted with giving a $1,000 grant to every poor person in America—all helped to make libertarian ideas a viable opposition force. In 1976, the Libertarian's candidate for governor in California gained 5 percent of the vote. Justin Raimondo claimed the party was poised for "exponential growth." But the Libertarian Party's self destructive habit of embracing a bizarre social agenda kept them in the less than 1 percent range.[3]

Rothbard and Fleming were natural allies. Both abhorred the welfare/warfare state. Neither man had any use for the establishment political parties. Both had been expelled from the ranks of polite company on the American right. Rothbard had been on the outside far longer than Fleming, but the latter, too, felt no self-pity over his banishment. In 1990, the Rockford and Von Mises people formed their own annual debating club, the John Randolph Society. Talks from these meetings made it to the pages of *Chronicles* and other publications. Rockwell and Rothbard often had their columns published in newspapers across the country, thus joining Buchanan, Francis, and Sobran on the op-ed pages.

As much as immigration, foreign policy thrust the Old Right into the spotlight. There was plenty on that front to keep them busy. With the end of the Cold War, the United States did not become, as Jeane Kirkpatrick had hoped, a "normal country living in normal times." Rather, it sought aggressively to expand its empire deep into Eastern Europe and into even the former republics of the Soviet Union. When the Soviet Empire was unraveling, Russian officials accepted the inevitable. They agreed to dissolve the Warsaw Pact. But while they did so, the Kremlin sought—and received—assurances from Washington and Bonn that NATO would not expand into their former satellite nations. Those promises didn't last long. President Bill Clinton's administration initially opposed NATO expansion, but the sirens of empire sounded too strongly for this former Vietnam War protestor to resist.

Equal in importance were the undeclared wars in Panama, Iraq, Bosnia, Haiti, Somalia, and Yugoslavia. Wondering if the American "experience" was truly conservative, M. E. Bradford had to make exceptions. "We have been a troublesome and unruly people from the beginning," Bradford admitted in a 1986 speech, "with little respect for legitimate authority and little appreciation for the keeping of right order or public service. We have exhibited a blind faith in technology or commercial ingenuity and in the value of mere mobility, with an indifference to what is providentially given in the human condition....Too often Americans have said in their hearts, 'You shall be as gods.'" As such, Americans have been a warlike people, too. Never more so was the case than when the U.S. wore the mantle of the world's "lone superpower." The 1991 war with Iraq marked the first time in the post-1945 era that leading conservative pundits—Buchanan, Sobran, Rowland Evans and Robert Novak—opposed a large-scale American military effort. The Old Right savaged Mr. Bush's war with more gusto than anything the antiwar left was capable of mustering, a fact that would catch the attention of such longtime leftists as Alexander Cockburn and Eugene Genovese.[4]

The Old Right consensus was that Iraq, despite its petty ruler and its invasion and occupation of Kuwait, was still a small country (a GNP the size of Kentucky) that posed no military threat to American interests anywhere in the world. Like Robert Taft, paleos are not pacifists. They favored keeping Saddam Hussein in a box where he could do no harm to his neighbors. Meanwhile, a negotiated settlement could force Iraq out of Kuwait. American military strength could further keep Saddam's imperial ambitions at bay. During the 1980s, the Reagan administration had informally backed Iraq in its bloody war with neighboring Iran. Toward this end, the U.S. sold military hardware to Saddam's regime. In 1991, however, the first shots were fired by the Bush administration. When Iraq invaded Kuwait in June 1990, President Bush originally adopted a containment policy towards the aggressors. American troops in Saudi Arabia were there strictly in a defensive posture, to keep Saddam from invading that oil-rich nation. But Margaret Thatcher lectured President Bush, reminding him that this was "no time to get wobbly." And so, Bush quickly made up his mind to bomb Iraq and invade Kuwait. American and British bombing runs excited the American public, but did not impress Old Right pundits. "What a country we have become," Fleming dryly observed, "with our patriotic songs and yellow ribbons commemorating something like a genocidal slaughter of a primitive people." Such criticism was echoed by Ross Perot, who claimed the war took place only because Mr. Bush's "manhood" had been threatened by Saddam Hussein.[5]

Old Right opposition to the Gulf War, as striking as it appeared, wasn't out of character. Paleos were skeptical about any military attempt to force Manuel Noriega out of power in Panama. Supporting the Contras battling the Soviet-backed Sandinistas was one thing. One could invoke the Monroe Doctrine. An eccentric tinpot like Noriega wasn't worth American blood anymore than the super-wealthy emirs in Kuwait.

As significant was Old Right opposition to American involvement in Yugoslavia's various civil wars that cropped up during the 1990s. In 1987, a longtime communist *appartchik*, Slobodan Milosevic, took power of that patchwork nation mainly by defending the tiny Serb minority from abuse by the Albanian majority in Yugoslavia's Kosovo province. In the late 1980s, Yugoslavia, with its Orthodox Christian, Roman Catholic, and Muslim populations experienced an outbreak of nationalism that began the eventual unraveling of the Soviet Empire. Yugoslavia saw several of its provinces—Croatia, Slovenia, and Bosnia—all attempt to break free, while in early 1999, the U.S. and Great Britain bombed that country for seventy-eight straight days and nights to end a civil war in Kosovo and place that province under NATO control. Buchanan opposed Milosevic's efforts to keep mostly Catholic Croatia part of Yugoslavia. He even suggested the U.S. move its Seventh Fleet into the Adriatic Sea as a show of strength designed to influence Milosevic's behavior. Croatia was an American ally in the Revolutionary War. That, too, counted for something. Buchanan, however, did not advocate American military action. Beyond that, the Old Right was united in its belief that the U.S. stay out of civil wars in Bosnia and Kosovo. Yugoslavia, with a population of ten million and suffering under 40 percent unemployment, was similar to Iraq in that it posed no military threat to the United States—or to London, Paris, Rome, and Berlin.

In Bosnia, the U.S. supported efforts by Muslims and Croats to form federations within the new majority-Serb nation. Eventually, Bosnia was partitioned into Serb, Muslim, and Croatian zones with NATO diplomats running the confederation. If the democratically-elected Serb parliament in Bosnia got out of line, then unelected NATO overseers would simply dissolve the entire body. During debates over Bosnia's future, Milosevic handed over Saravejo to NATO's military men, all in a "good faith" gesture, which also allowed him to keep power back home.

In Kosovo, however, Milosevic could not hand over that province to NATO. Kosovo was mostly Albanian, but it was also sacred ground for the Serbs. Northern Kosovo was the site of a 1389 battle between the Serbs and Turkish invaders. There, a beloved Serb leader, Prince Lazar, fought and died with his outnumbered Serb troops. While the Albanians converted to Islam (the triumphant Turks' religion), the conquered Serbs remained Christian. The *Wall Street Journal*, in particular, sneered at the notion that a fourteenth-century battle should still move late-twentieth-century peoples. But the boys at the *Journal* could also not understand why some Americans would not want land next to the Manassas Battlefield turned into a Disney theme park. In 1940, Kosovo had a slim Serbian majority. During World War II, while the Serbs fought the Nazis, the Albanians sided with Hitler's forces, killing tens of thousands of Serbs in the process, and driving thousands more out of Kosovo. After the war, the Yugoslav dictator Marshall Tito, a man who always disliked Serbian nationalism, refused to allow displaced Serbs back into Kosovo. These tensions all simmered over in the late 1990s, when Kosovo became embroiled in its own civil war between Serbs and Albanians. NATO's Rambuillet, France accords (signed only by the Albanian guerrillas) stipulated that Yugoslavia, after three years, allow a vote on Kosovo independence. Furthermore, NATO troops would be allowed to travel anywhere they wished in Yugoslavia. Such troops could occupy the country without any resistance. Here was imperialism at its most arrogant.

Since Milosevic could not give up Kosovo, NATO bombs soon rained down on Yugoslavia. The province was quickly emptied out in a matter of days, creating Europe's worst refugee crisis since World War II. Eventually a peace deal was signed which, nominally at least, kept Kosovo part of Yugoslavia. NATO forces moved in for what would certainly be a decades-long occupation of that little province. The ethnic cleansing didn't end, either. Returning Albanians chased Serbs, Gypsies, and Jews out of Kosovo and into Serbia. Now, Serbian homes and Christian churches were being burnt, while Bill Clinton and Tony Blair looked the other way and CNN television cameras were nowhere to be found.

Paleos held no brief for Milosevic. His stirring defense of the Serb minority aside, Milosevic was simply another cunning, calculating master politician. Srdja Trifkovic, a Serbian native and *Chronicles* editor, slammed Milosevic as a power-hungry communist who, as noted, sold out his fellow Serbs in Bosnia simply to curry favor with NATO and hold onto power in Belgrade. Still, Old Right criticism of Clinton's Yugoslav war reached new rhetorical heights. "Sadistic" (Trifkovic), "cowardly" (McConnell) were just two choice adjectives. Fleming, meanwhile, opined that "only a civilized people [the U.S. State Department] are capable of such lying and savagery." The Yugoslav war, McConnell claimed, was also a "civilizational" conflict. Bombs from American and British jets hit Christian churches (some going back to the eighth century), plus schools, hospitals, and factories. Civilians were maimed and killed, hundreds of thousands of able-bodied men with families to support were thrown out of work when their factories were destroyed. One errant NATO bomb even hit the Chinese embassy, killing several diplomats. Another struck a truck filled with Albanian refugees, an error that NATO officials first denied, then acknowledged.[6]

Why oppose an American Empire? The U.S. government does not advertise itself as such. America is not as explicit in its intentions as the Romans or the British once were. But the State Department and the intelligence agencies seek to control the internal affairs of every nation it can, if possible, every nation on earth. This includes economic policies, whom nations must elect as their leaders, the right of the U.S. to interfere in various civil wars, and even promoting birth control measures, including abortion. The U.S. has troops in upwards of 100 countries, all with no congressional or certainly, no public opposition in sight. There, first, is the matter of America's destiny. The U.S., as paleos have claimed for decades, was only meant to be a constitutional republic, not an empire—as Buchanan's 1999 foreign policy tome nostalgically states. Republics mind their own business. Their governments have very limited powers, and their people are too busy practicing self-government to worry about problems in other countries. Empires not only bully smaller, defenseless nations, they also can't leave their own hapless subjects alone—another stubborn fact of life that has long animated Old Right opposition to the garrison state. A national government that wants certain people in power in nations as different as Iraq, Somalia, Bosnia, Haiti, and Yugoslavia isn't going to allow people in Alabama or Kansas to control the destinies of their own local governments. Empires and the tenth amendment aren't friends.

There are many other costs to an empire, including the obvious ones to the taxpayer. The welfare state is bad, all conservatives agree. Such programs result in higher taxes, an unfair redistribution of wealth from working people to able-bodied dependencies. The welfare state increases the size and power of the centralized regime. The warfare state has the same characteristics. Americans see their tax dollars wasted on foreign aid, on American troops not only in the prosperous nations of Western Europe, but, as noted, all around the world. There is also the matter of Cold War defense budgets in a post-1989 world. On a radio talk show, I once heard a young lady complaining about the astronomical "peacetime" taxes she and her fellow Americans are paying. As any Old Rightists could tell her, Americans do not pay peacetime taxes. They pay wartime taxes—and will continue doing so for the foreseeable future.

An empire represents the ultimate consolidation of power. It stands opposed to the regional cultures paleos cherish. Culture, too, must be centralized. Let the people be entertained instead by the junk flowing from Manhattan and Hollywood. Empire also means government policies conducted in secrecy: Bureaucrats at the State Department, the C.I.A., the Pentagon, and the National Security Council all know what's best for the public; that same public doesn't need to know about the operations of such agencies. And so, an empire cannot tolerate any dissent, from the pols to the pundits to the masses alike. There were, for instance, full-scale campaigns to have newspapers all across the country drop the syndicated columns of both Pat Buchanan and Joe Sobran once those two came out against the Gulf War—proving that things hadn't changed since Flynn and Garrett challenged the war party in the 1930s and 1940s. The Cato Institute, a leading libertarian think tank, had long enjoyed funding by the Olin, Scaife, and Smith-Richardson foundations. Once Cato came out against Mr. Bush's war, the Olin Foundation cut off all funding to that think tank. Cato's opposition was deemed "unpatriotic," proving these libertarians were unworthy of further funds. In all, empires make a mockery not only of America's long-lost republican traditions, but also of its still-smoldering democratic ones. "National greatness" conservatives who want a strong U.S. military presence abroad and limited government at home are probably fooling themselves—if indeed, they are even serious about the latter proposition. Empires and small government aren't compatible, either.[7]

Most serious of all, empires create endless enemies. Such a claim seemed insignificant to Americans at the dawn of the millennium. The American empire is triumphant, unchallenged, complete with air wars, military occupation, and the expansion of NATO into Poland,

Hungary, and the Czech Republic. No one can imagine the U.S. losing a war, much less even fighting one on the ground. But paleos take the long view. The very long view. Empires don't last forever, even in an age of rapid technological advances, such as the deployment of missile defense systems designed to defend America from a foreign missile attack. The world's peoples do not like—nor have they ever liked—one nation being so dominant. They eventually rise up against their foreign rulers. Plus, modern technology works both ways. It means more advanced weapons, but also rogue nations building those same weapons for their own uses. Throughout the 1990s, Iran, for instance, worked to develop nuclear weapons. Two nonaligned Asian nations, India and Pakistan, tested nuclear weapons. Both nations have a long history of ill will towards each other over border disputes, but for India at least there were other factors. After the Gulf War, an Indian defense minister returned home to declare the meaning of that war: A nation had better develop and test nuclear weapons if it does not want to be attacked by the United States—an embarrassing commentary on how at least the world's soon-to-be most populous nation viewed Uncle Sam. There was more. Ending decades of frosty relationships, Russia and China improved economic and military ties. Still sore over America's expansion of NATO, Russia sold valuable weapons technology to Iran. China aided Russia during the latter's civil war in Chechnya. (The Clinton administration, for its part, had tried giving material aid to the Chechan rebels.) The inevitable challenges to American hegemony had begun. In the wake of Kosovo, anti-NATO sentiment ran high in both the streets of Europe and, less frantically, among many European statesmen. European leaders began discussing the formation of a Western European Union (WEU) to serve as a military arm of the more economically inclined European Union. Equally nervous Americans worried that this might mean the eventual end of the NATO alliance. Even Great Britain expressed sympathy for a new European security force, one totally free of American control.

A world turned upside down, indeed. In the late 1980s, the Soviet Union was the Evil Empire, the U.S. still a shining, if troubled, light of the West. A decade later, Washington had broken its word to Moscow about NATO expansion. In addition, the administration of George W. Bush was determined to work toward a missile defense construction, one that would violate the 1972 ABM treaty. Relations with Russia, which seemed promising at the beginning of the decade, continued to disintegrate. This development, however, caused little consternation among the Beltway ruling class.

There, too, was the clash of civilizations. More than ever, America's elites in education, big business, the media, the government, the publishing and entertainment industries alike, all embraced anti-Western, anti-Christian ideologies such as multiculturalism, plus such totalitarian measures as political correctness. Meanwhile, Russia, to some Old Rightists, was seen as a poor, corruption-riddled country that nonetheless had a fighting chance of regaining its Orthodox Christian heritage, one laid low by decades of communist rule. Russian schoolchildren opened and ended their day with a prayer, while in the United States, school prayer, even at high school football games, was met with the usual hostility. Where was Western civilization now?

As troubling to Old Rightists was the knee-jerk American policy of economic sanctions. Both the left and right wielded the sanctions sword. In the 1980s, liberals liked to use it against South Africa, the Philippines, El Salvador, and other "right wing" bad guys. Conservatives did the same to communist regimes in Nicaragua and Poland. Both sides agreed that Castro's Cuba must labor under sanctions, even after the Soviet Union fell and Castro's totalitarian regime was no longer fomenting Marxist revolution in Central and South America. Economic sanctions, as Murray Rothbard long claimed, are an act of war, an example of one nation trying to starve and cripple another through non-military means. By its second term, the hawkish (and highly moralistic) Clinton administration had leveled sanctions against over thirty nations—none of whom could pose a military threat to the U.S.

Most significant were American sanctions against Iraq. President Bush, as Pat Buchanan recalled, declared America's enemy to be Saddam Hussein, not the Iraqi people. It didn't turn out that way. After America's massive bombing war ended in the spring of 1991, Saddam remained in power, as did American sanctions against that country—in place because Hussein had allegedly violated terms of the peace agreement. The 1990s saw enormous suffering in Iraq. United Nations estimates put the death toll of innocents at one million, mainly through malnutrition and lack of medical supplies. Iraqi children were among the casualties: Anywhere from 100,000 to 500,000 of those one million dead were thought to be young children. Saddam, U.S. officials maintained, was part of the problem. The Iraqi dictator used monies from oil exports for weapons or weapons savings, rather than for foodstuffs. But American-led sanctions hardly eased the suffering. The *San*

Jose Mercury News reported that in some instances, upwards of 4,000 Iraqi children were dying *per week*. Eventually, other nations had seen enough of the Bush/Clinton sanctions policy. The French, the Russians, and the Chinese, among other nations, began ignoring the Yanks and Brits by flying their own foodstuffs and other material things into Iraq. The consequences of such sanctions was not just the loss of America's moral standing in the world. The pro-Washington coalition of European and Arab countries, fashioned by the Bush administration to fight Iraq, had fallen apart. The ongoing sanctions war had created even greater bitterness toward the U.S. on the "Arab street."[8]

On the frontlines, the situation went from perilous to catastrophic. The American empire was neither cost nor blood-free. Ivan Elan of the Cato Institute chronicled the terrorist attacks—and near misses—against American troops and installations both abroad and at home. In both Lebanon in 1983 and in Somalia, ten years later, the deaths of American servicemen from either terrorist bombs or firefights with local militias drove U.S. military personnel from those small nations. Americans will pay the price of empire in dollars, including billions for "peacekeeping" forces in the Balkans. They will not, in these times of low birth rates, pay the price in blood. Also, in the 1980s, Ronald Reagan and Libyan dictator, Muommar El-Quadaffi, engaged in a periodic war of words and weaponry. In 1986, the U.S. retaliated for the Libyan bombing of a German nightclub (which killed an American solider) by bombing two Libyan cities. Two years later, an American Pan Am 103 airliner was blown up over Scotland. Needless to say, there were plenty of suspects, including Quadaffi. By 1998, Quadaffi had turned over two Libyan subjects to Western authorities—and promptly got all international sanctions against his regime lifted. The Clinton administration was plagued not only by Somali, but also by embassy bombings in Saudi Arabia, Kenya, and Tanzania. By the end of the 1990s, sixty-six American embassies around the world were shut down, with the State Department declaring four out of five of all such buildings unsafe for operations. The biggest potential disaster was represented by the 1993 World Trade Center bombing. Here, the immigration crisis collided with planned terrorism against Americans. The suspects were in the U.S. on green card visas ("for jobs that should have gone to Americans," as Thomas Fleming protested). The suspects—like hundreds of thousands of other legal-turned-illegal aliens—had overstayed their visas with dastardly acts in mind to boot. Their ultimate goal failed— the sodium cyanide planted with the converted bomb burned rather than vaporized—and so, the casualty count was only five dead Americans. Had it succeeded, up to 50,000 innocent Americans would have died in an explosion targeted to destroy two of the largest buildings in the world.[9]

Then, eight years later, it happened. On September 11, 2001, the nightmare scenario actually took place. Again, the immigrant/terrorist fuse exploded. On that morning, nineteen Middle Eastern nationals, all of whom had legally entered the United States hijacked four passenger planes. Two of them hit the World Trade Center and one attacked the Pentagon. Over 3,000 people, mostly Americans, perished. U.S. authorities immediately fingered Osama bin Laden as the mastermind behind the attacks. An angry nation called for war, and President Bush quickly sent warships and bombers to bases in Pakistan as a prelude for full-scale war against Afghanistan, the nation which harbored bin Laden and elements of his Al Qaeda network.

The terrorist bombings highlighted an intense resentment that existed against the U.S. throughout not just the Arab world, but much of the planet as well. Naturally, such sentiments became a cause for debate. The pundit class quickly dismissed the uproar as simple jealously for American notions of freedom, and democracy, plus its materialistic way of life. Old Right columnists, typically enough, took a dissenting view. Since the end of the Cold War, the powerful American military had bombed and invaded poor nations on four continents. Plus, there was the stationing of American troops on Arab land, especially Saudi Arabia. Nothing could justify the evil acts of September 11. But aggressive American behavior, especially its bombing runs and economic sanctions, had sowed the seeds of large-scale resentment.

Throughout the passions incited by the new war, Old Rightists calmly advocated a foreign policy they claimed was in the true American tradition. Specifically, one first enunciated by George Washington and Thomas Jefferson: No entangling alliances, combined with good will and commerce with all nations. This would mean the end of American tax dollars for not just the United Nations, but also NATO, the World Trade Organization, and the International Monetary Fund. The U.S. would give aid to victims of civil strife or natural disasters, but it would not chose sides in conflicts that had no bearing on American interests (a civil war in Mexico might catch Washington's attention). The Old Right had sympathy for a doctrine first articulated in the 1960s by Arkansas Senator William J. Fulbright, himself an early critic of the Vietnam War: The United States has no quarrel with the government of any foreign nation, provided that said government does not threaten America.[10] Paleos could only hope that it would not take more wars or even greater catastrophes for the country to adopt a more prudent foreign policy. A nation might not have any friends in this world; the least it can do is not make enemies.

7

What the Old Right is For

Preceding chapters have discussed what paleoconservatives are against, what they dislike about the American regime that triumphed in the twentieth century. On that, there is much unity. Still, Old Right thinkers, in the manner of conservatives in opposing camps, have quarreled amongst themselves. Disagreements did not occur over foreign policy, immigration, tax and spending, or social issues. Rather, the issue that divided the Old Right was trade. Von Mises Institute scholars opposed both the North American Free Trade Agreement (NAFTA) and the more ambitious General Agreement on Trade and Tariffs (GATT) on grounds that both treaties would create huge multinational bureaucracies to manage a so-called free trade. Plus, there was the sovereignty issue. The NAFTA deal included the creation of a panel of Canadian, American, and Mexican bureaucrats who would decide environmental policy and laws for those three nations. With GATT, trade disputes would be the domain not of the nations involved and their legislative bodies, but of yet another panel of bureaucratic wise men. In the late 1990s, for instance, the U.S. Congress passed legislation, signed into law by President Clinton, that restricted off-shore fishing in the Pacific Ocean. Japan and several other Asian nations protested, taking their case to the World Trade Organization. The WTO ruled in favor of the protesting nations and the law of a sovereign nation, in this case, the United States, was nullified. The U.S. Constitution states that only Congress can make the laws Americans live under. However, the boys at the WTO weren't listening. Again, all factions of the Old Right were in agreement. Paleolibertarians were not globalists; as much as the paleocons, they opposed one-world notions, whether they lived at the UN, NATO, the IMF, or the WTO.

But the Von Mises people strongly supported the idea of free trade and free markets. Trade was also where Buchanan made his mark as a national political figure. After the 1992 elections, Ross Perot with his 19 million votes was in a much stronger position to lead the budding populism movement. One 1993 poll even had Perot defeating Bill Clinton in a two-man race by a 46-33 percent margin. Perot also opposed NAFTA. But after performing poorly in a nationally televised debate with Al Gore on the issue, the Texan pretty much dropped out of the political process, making only a half-hearted run in 1996. Buchanan, however, was only too happy to carry the populist banner. A free trader in the Reagan White House, Buchanan's meetings during the 1992 campaign with manufacturing workers worried about losing their jobs, plus his earlier unhappiness with 1980s trade scandals involving Japan and The Netherlands (both countries had sold sensitive military technology to the Soviet Union), all moved him to his "trade hawk" position. Free and fair trade with Canada, Great Britain, and Germany, nations whose working wages are on par with those of America's are fine. But free trade with Mexico and nations whose manufacturing wages are far below American standards, is unacceptable. American auto workers, for instance, make up to $40 an hour, plus they receive generous health and retirement benefits, all the result of hard-won gains made by previous generations of trade union activists. In Mexico, however, the same job can be performed for less than a dollar an hour, with no side benefits. Plus, Mexico does not impose the same strict environmental standards on manufacturers as Washington does. Following NAFTA's passage in 1993, auto plants sprang up like mushrooms on the Mexican side of the border. Meanwhile, in both the 1980s and 1990s alone, up to four million manufacturing jobs left the United States.

There was also the matter of wages. This, not low unemployment, zero inflation or even the booming stock market, was the real economic story from the early 1970s onward. Starting in the 1970s, wage increases could not keep pace with inflation. From 1972 to 1994, wages dropped 19 percent. Not just the downward pressure on wages created by the immigrant labor pool, but also the loss of millions of good-paying manufacturing jobs were forces bedeviling American working families. Wages did begin increasing in the mid-1990s—but only for female workers. For male workers, wages continued their decades-long plunge.

Rothbard tolerated Buchanan's apostasy on free trade; he pleaded with his skeptical colleagues that any man is due one failing, and for

Buchanan, it was free trade. Otherwise, he was their man, not only the most anti-statist candidate, but also the only one capable of restoring America's republican heritage. Rothbard held high hopes for the rejuvenated Old Right of the 1990s. With *Chronicles* as the intellectual monthly, *Human Events* as a feisty weekly and Buchanan as a charismatic, articulate leader, the Old Right could leave both the Buckleyites and the neoconservatives in the dust while on their way to revolutionizing American politics. However, after Rothbard's untimely death in December 1994, the John Randolph Club coalition fell apart. At its 1996 meeting, University of Nevada professor Hans-Herbert Hoppe delivered a stinging criticism of Buchanan's trade protectionism. In doing so, he also attacked Sam Francis, not by name, but by criticizing excerpts of his writings. Given Francis's distinctive prose style, audience members knew exactly who Hoppe was lambasting.

And so, the Von Mises contingent was no longer part of these get-togethers. But there was no clear break between the two factions. Paleolibertarians still wrote for *Chronicles*. In addition, Von Mises, beginning in the mid-90s, organized several groundbreaking conferences of their own, the papers from which were collected in hard-hitting volumes, written in the hell-for-leather style that distinguishes the Old Right. *The Costs of War*, published in 1997, is one of the most ambitious Old Right projects. Arguing that America's "Pyrrhic victories" in its numerous wars have only resulted in a larger, more restrictive government, less freedom, and fewer civil liberties, the volume especially singled out World War I as the modern era's great global catastrophe. Here was the war that marked the beginning of the end of a classical European civilization, while, in the states, it saw the inauguration of wartime programs that would serve as the model for FDR's New Deal. Other interesting insights included Allan Carlson's contention that World War II dramatically changed America's moral codes, especially relations between young men and women. Once American soldiers were exposed to the decadent social norms in Europe, Africa, and Asia those men would not return to the old-fashioned ways of courtship and marriage still demanded by American women. Thanks to World War II, a *Playboy*-style culture was already in ascendancy by the late 1940s. Sam Francis touched on a familiar theme, noticing that modern-day American and British governments practiced a militaristic foreign policy abroad, while also seeking to disarm their own subjects at home through draconian gun control measures. Finally, Murray Rothbard declared that the Revolutionary War and the war between the states represented the only two "just wars" in American history: that is, wars where a people fight in self-defense to "rid themselves of an unwanted domination by another people."[1]

Thoughts on secession tackled another controversial issue; one made relevant by the breakup of the Soviet Union, Czechoslovakia, Yugoslavia, and secession movements in Canada, India, and various European nations. Again, the paleolibertarians went against the grain. They did not call for secession anywhere, but they defended such actions as bids for liberation, not thoughtless rebellion. Political divorce was often seen as a way to assure not just old-fashioned liberties, but the integrity of traditional cultures. The contributors also reiterated that secession was an American tradition. The thirteen colonies, after all, seceded from Great Britain. New York and Virginia both refused to join the new union unless they received guarantees that they could secede at any time. During the early decades of the republic, the threat of secession was made over a variety of issues: the Louisiana Purchase, the national embargo of 1807, early non-British immigration, the Alien and Sedition Acts, the War of 1812, the "abominable" tariffs of the early 1830s, and the Mexican War—all before the event actually took place in 1861. As a result, the volume was sympathetic towards not only the old Confederacy, but also the secession movement in Quebec. Essayists also waxed nostalgic over a European continent that once consisted of thousands of free cities, small monarchies, and other independent political entities. Or as Joe Sobran has observed, when Europe was made up of "only" 500 political units, no Hitler or Stalin could rise among them. There were no superstates that might swallow up smaller, poorer ones. Contributors saw real benefits from such a radical devolution. The indefatigable Rothbard championed wholesale privatization as the way to achieve a harmonious and prosperous social order. Clyde Wilson claimed that "multiple and dispersed sovereignty" in small communities would lead to "creativity in wealth, art, intellect, and every other good thing."[2]

Continuing in the same spirit, a 1998 Von Mises seminar on the American presidency examined the debasement of that once-noble office. Presidents were once mere executives, signing or vetoing congressional legislation. The Founding Fathers, as a Von Mises flyer recalled, "tried to make sure that presidents could not tax, spend or make war on their own." With Lincoln, Wilson, FDR, Truman, and LBJ as the main culprits, the office was now home to arrogant, ill-tempered warmongers, wreaking death and destruction abroad and practicing, through undemocratic means, tyranny at home. "The U.S. presidency," the Von Mises people stated, "hosts the tax police, the gun grabbers, the land seizers, the race baiters, the business wreckers, and the secret police....It runs the entire global welfare-warfare state."[3]

In an age of any American president as "the most powerful man in the world," James Burnham once argued for Congress to take its stand as a legislative body capable of checking executive branch excesses. Up until the 1950s and the Korean War, presidents understood that only Congress could declare war. However, by the 1980s, conservatives were complaining about "535 Secretaries of States" thwarting Ronald Reagan's Central American policy. Foreign policy, many conservatives now claimed, was the domain of the executive branch. Congress should stay out of such matters, even though that branch, under the Constitution, could only appropriate the money to support the Contra guerrilla army cause so important to the right. It was the idea of a president as the most powerful man in the world that the Old Right utterly rejected. Who needs it? Such a figure suggests a modern-day Julius Caesar raining down terror on unruly subjects all over the globe. It did not matter that Milosevic's Yugoslavia posed no military threat to the United States. The recalcitrant Serbs needed to be taught a lesson. A world-emperor is exactly where the office of Washington and Jefferson had landed.[4]

Although the politics of the 1990s were overshadowed by the endless Clinton scandals, they still held monumental importance for the nation's future. A December 22, 1997 article in the *Christian Science Monitor* neatly capsulated the new era. American politics, the publication correctly claimed, was no longer a matter of liberal vs. conservative, but rather globalists vs. nationalists. The article was accompanied by a color photograph of a grinning Bill Clinton walking along the White House grounds, trailed by an equally pleased Newt Gingrich. Both men appeared to be on their way to a bill-signing ceremony. The photo was highly symbolic, portraying the leading globalists of the 1990s in apparent agreement on another issue. The two weren't alone. The whole globalists vs. nationalists showdown was a huge mismatch, with all the firepower on the globalists' side.[5]

A free trade-open immigration borders-interventionist foreign policy complemented by the ever-growing federal government they created was pursued with a religious fervor by elites on both the left and right. Globalists could count on the liberal news media (the *New York Times,* the *Washington Post, Time, Newsweek,* the *New Republic*); their conservative brethren (the *Wall Street Journal,* the *Washington Times,* the *American Spectator, National Review*, and the Rush Limbaugh program); retired statesmen (Gerald Ford, Jimmy Carter, Henry Kissinger, James A. Baker, Howard Baker); and the new computer-driven business class as exemplified by Bill Gates all for support whenever push came to shove on key issues. Throughout his presidency, Clinton could rely on Gingrich, Bob Dole and the rest of the Republican leadership to back him on trade legislation, such as NAFTA, GATT, and free trade deals for various Caribbean and African nations.

Badly outnumbered on the other side was Buchanan, the erstwhile Ross Perot, and Richard Gephart, a lawmaker not so much opposed to globalism as he was for union and environmental rights in countries with which America was hoping to conclude free trade agreements. The longtime leftist publication, the *Nation*, remained skeptical about one world economics. Other liberals, such as Ralph Nader and his Green Party, campaigned hardily against the excesses of multinational corporations. However, both the *Nation* and the editors at *Chronicles* received little notice from the mainstream media. *Human Events* also opposed certain free trade deals and expressed doubts about several post-Cold War military adventures, as well. But as with immigration, *HE's* criticism was muted, as the publication remained wedded to supporting the Republican Party. Meanwhile, the Democratic Party's tried to regain its congressional majority through trade protection. Boosted by vital AFL-CIO money, the Democrats, in 1997, rallied to defeat President Clinton's attempt to gain fast track legislation needed for more free trade deals. Both Clinton and Vice President Al Gore were free traders, but only a diminishing number of Democrats in Congress subscribed to a trade theory that their party, beginning in the 1940s, had championed strongly throughout the postwar era.

In the great debate, Old Rightists support an enlightened nationalism, one based on complete fidelity to national sovereignty. Nationalism can be a misleading term. Most paleos generally dislike it. Nationalist sentiments have often led to warlike behavior. The Old Right does not support a militant nationalism designed to enlarge the federal government. Furthermore, Fleming counsels against a nationalism that scapegoats ethnic or racial minorities, one that is built on hatred of "the other" rather than on love of one's own culture, history, and heritage. There are some functions a national government has for its own, ones that may even result in some good. Foreign policy is the most obvious. Congress controls the purse strings. Only that body can declare war. In addition, it can prevent military action by cutting off the expenditures for such plans. Trade is another issue where Congress can show some backbone.

Intellectual movements are hard to pin down, especially when a herd of freethinking individuals are involved. Paleoconservatism represents a mixture of nationalism and regionalism. Opposition to free trade means preventing good-paying manufacturing jobs from going overseas. Many an American community is built around industries such as steel and textiles. Cities and towns that have lost such jobs—Detroit, Buffalo, Gary, Youngstown, Weirton, West Virginia—have in turn, lost tens of thousands (in Detroit's case, millions) of residents, leaving them as mere shells of their once-confident selves. The entire wage stagnation discussed earlier has had devastating social consequences as well. When cities lose industries, family ties are severed. Young people must seek work elsewhere. In addition, young couples cannot afford to have many children; birth rates in America have dropped 50 percent since the baby boom years of the 1950s and 1960s. Even with one child to support, both parents must work, forcing Junior to spend his formative years in impersonal day care centers.

For the Old Right, successful policies result in government activities being kept close to home. An America First foreign policy not only keeps the country out of unnecessary wars; by bringing the troops home, it also saves the taxpayer a goodly amount of money. Best of all, it decreases the size and power of the government in Washington, as do other revolutionary actions, especially those concerning domestic issues. The Old Right not only dislikes the programs and spirit of the New Deal and the Great Society, but also such seemingly harmless offspring, including the Interstate Highway System (ruins small towns by making them accessible to would-be suburbanites who move there in large numbers, thus obliterating that same small-town character); mandatory education laws (takes kids out of the house at an early age and puts them under the influence of strangers preaching alien ideologies); and the military life in general (families are uprooted, moved from base to base, divorce and family breakups often follow).[6]

Regionalism is a way of making sense out of life on the continental-sized American land mass. It represents the celebration of a diversity worth saving. When Donald Davidson, in the 1930s, wrote of the "diversity of America," he mostly meant regional cultures that endured in New England, the South, the Midwest, and the Western states, not shrill ideologies based on race, ethnicity, language, and gender. Furthermore, the tenth amendment serves as the lodestar for dealing with controversial social issues. Let the states and localities decide on abortion, school prayer, pornography, and other matters where culture and politics collide. The gun debate, another issue that spooks the Beltway Right, is also better left to the states. By the mid-90s, over thirty states had enacted concealed weapons laws, allowing citizens, in the Jeffersonian tradition, to "let a gun be their companion," that is, to carry firearms for protection outside the home. Federal judges in some Western states ruled that "Brady Bill" gun control measures (which imposed a waiting period on gun sales) were unconstitutional. Liberals responded by agitating for more federal gun laws, including a national ID program for all gun owners, a step on the way to making all handgun purchases illegal. Soon, the gun issue proved to be one of the most divisive issues separating rural from urban America.

Laws are based on cultural beliefs. Paramount among cultural characteristics is religion. Sober Old Right thinkers do not claim that all of America is a Christian nation. There is too much evidence to suggest otherwise. Still, large portions of America are guided by traditional Christian ethics. If, say, Louisiana, Utah, and Pennsylvania are pro-life states, then it reflects the religious cultures of those entities: Louisiana and Pennsylvania with their unique mix of conservative Catholics and Protestants, and Utah with its Mormon foundation. Likewise, Alabama is probably the most pro-school prayer state in America. In many Alabama counties, up to 80 percent of all residents attend church on Sunday. In addition, mere common sense, as Fleming has often pointed out, once served as a guide to prudent lawmaking. If folks out West or in upstate New York oppose gun control, it's because of their rural residence. This makes it difficult for police to answer security concerns. There is also the manly duty of protecting one's family and property. Firearms ownership is second nature to most rural and small-town Americans. Likewise, the abundance of wide-open roads accompanied by few drivers makes those same Westerners support a sixty-five mile per hour speed limit. On the other hand, drivers on the congested highways in the urban Northeast would prefer the speed limit to remain at fifty-five MPH. Either way, the focus must be away from the "national government" James Madison warned against in *The Federalist Papers*.

Legalities aside, the Old Right makes its own robust celebration of the nation's regional cultures, championing them as the nation's very lifeblood. On the pages of *Chronicles*, the clarion call issued by Davidson back in the 1930s was sounded again. Rockford's location in

the Midwest comes in handy here. The Beltway Right does not completely ignore Middle America. Editors at *Human Events* swear fidelity to heartland concerns. The *Weekly Standard*, under William Kristol's
sometimes pragmatic editorship, will publish articles supportive of that
same school prayer movement in Alabama; it will also praise the career of Merle Haggard and the achievement of country music in general. The literature of the American West is given a thoughtful hearing.
But like most East Coast, right-of-center journals, Republican Party
politics and the doings on Capitol Hill and 1600 Pennsylvania Avenue
remain the major concern. The Old Right, on the other hand, wants to
build a Middle America-based cultural movement that will force politicians to dance to a populist tune.

So let's look at examples of these defiant calls for a rebirth of re-
gional cultures. For beginners, there is Chilton Williamson, Jr. on a
Western states culture that exists even among the ruins of modern
America:

> [While] most of the nation has wandered off into the postindustrial age, in the
> rural Mountain West, the preindustrial era survives...Westerners tend not to
> be...specialists: they are likely instead to have knowledge and skills to be compe-
> tent in many jobs beyond their paid line of work, such as operating a backhoe,
> repairing a truck engine, building a house, shoeing a horse, cutting cows and sort-
> ing sheep, killing and butchering domestic animals and big game; felling trees.
> Their versatility makes them self-reliant and self-reliance keeps them indepen-
> dent, without precluding the cooperativeness whose absence makes frontier life
> impossible.[7]

Sometimes the defense of regionalism is nostalgic, an effort to remind Americans of a lost heritage. In this case, there is Allan Carlson
on the agrarian Midwest:

> James "Tama Jim" Wilson...United States Secretary of Agriculture for a record 16
> years, said about [the] Midwest, "There was never a country so rich as this. There
> was never a country so prosperous....There was never a people so contended as
> ours.... A new dignity has come to agriculture, along with its economic strength,
> and the farmer has a new horizon...which is more promising than the skyline of the
> city."...Average farm size in Iowa was one hundred and fifty-one acres in 1890,
> and 151.2 in 1900, suggesting no trend toward consolidation. Farm technology
> was stable, resting still on true horse power, and prices for farm commodities were
> relatively good. Small towns blossomed across the landscape....[From] 1900 to as
> late as 1980, Iowa would claim, in absolute terms, more incorporated towns of
> under a thousand people than any other in the union.[8]

Swinging southward, there is Michael Hill on the virtues of the Old
South versus the crass materialism and moral cowardice of the New

South. The occasion was the 1996 Summer Olympics in Atlanta. Does the Old South cave into the demands of globalists now invading Dixie?

> In order to spare the feelings of international visitors, the Atlanta city fathers....went all out to banish every vestige of the Old Confederacy, including the Georgia state flag, which contains in its design the Confederate battleflag....But traditional Southerners fought the international octopus in their own small ways. A lawsuit was filed against the Atlanta suburb of Roswell, which forced the city to allow Confederate reenactors to march in a parade escorting the Olympic flame. In the rural north Alabama hamlet of Battleground, named in honor of General Nathan Bedford Forrest's victory at Day's Gap in 1863, city officials were asked to remove the battleflag that waves over the volunteer fire station on Highway 159 so as not to offend the bearer of the sacred flame. The local Bubbas reacted by hoisting two additional flags over the roadside plaque commemorating Forrest's triumph. "Them 'lympic folks ain't gonna tell us what to do," one retorted.[9]

Finally, there is Bill Kauffman, the upstate New York patriot, and most ambitious of all the Old Right regionalists. His 1989 novel, *Every Man A King*, tells the story of a young congressional aide turned conservative columnist who is forced out of Washington, D.C. only to find contentment among the blue-collar class in his upstate New York hometown. So devoted is Kauffman to upstate literature that he once quipped "he'd gladly read the entire Sinclairville phonebook." He happily compares his corner of western New York to the state's dominant Manhattanite cultural icons. "I'll gladly pit Edmund Wilson against Alfred Kazin," he claims, "William Kennedy against Jimmy Breslin, John Gardner against Philip Roth, Joyce Carol Oates against any New Yorker miniaturist, and, in the historical novelist category, Walter Edmonds against Arthur Schlesinger, Jr."[10]

Concerning politics, Kauffman is equally defiant. In the early 1970s, upstaters engaged in a popular, but futile attempt to secede from the rest of New York. Organizers had enough signatures for a referendum, but typically enough for New York politics, tens of thousands were declared ineligible, and the movement died a quiet death. Still, upstaters have a political heritage worth advancing:

> Division of New York is in the national interest because it would permit a new generation of upstatesmen to take the stage. We did...give America Martin Van Buren and Grover Cleveland...Barber Conable...a man of republican virtue and rectitude, would've made a fine President...The rural Democracy is populist, anti-bureaucracy and Green... Give us our own state and we just might give America another Bob Taft or William Jennings Bryan.[11]

Before television, Western culture was greatly shaped by the written word. American literature presents a dazzling array of regional products. And so, *Chronicles* would publish essays emphasizing the traditionalism of the New Englander Robert Frost, Westerners Edward Abbey and J. Evetts Haley, and such largely forgotten Midwestern novelists as Louis Bromfield and Glenway Wescott. With the exception of Abbey and Haley, all were artists who made their mark in the 1930s and 1940s, an era when the Manhattan publishing world still had conservative elements sympathetic toward Middle American sensibilities. Kauffman's 1995 book, *America First!* hailed such antiwar authors such as Abbey, Hamlin Garland, Amos Pinchot, Sinclair Lewis, and Gore Vidal, all of whom loved the old America that existed before the triumphant welfare-warfare state. In the post-World War II era, a different literature appealed to the new America. Novelists such as John Updike, John Cheever, Saul Bellow, Philip Roth, and Norman Mailer, plus postmodernists Thomas Pynchon and John Barth, were all popular among a college-educated middle class which prided itself on having no small amount of intellectual sophistication. Characters in such novels were often white-collar professionals, the setting, either the suburbs or the city; the focus middle-class angst, usually on how to live a moral life amidst this new, often complex American landscape. These novelists were favorites of East Coast-based publishers and reviewers. Their works usually went straight to the best seller lists. Some saw their visage on the cover of *Time* or *Newsweek*.

Rockford's T.S. Eliot Award for Creative Writing or its Richard M. Weaver Award for Scholarly Letters would be awarded to other types of writers. Kirk, Lytle, Forrest McDonald, Shelby Foote, Wendell Berry, and Fred Chappell, artists who either celebrated the old, eighteenth- and nineteenth-century America in their scholarship, or who carried on the agrarian tradition earlier dramatized by Frost and Faulkner, would be honored. Instead of dealing with the anxieties of an urban, technological order, such a literature expressed grave concern over the future of a culture informed more by an inherited oral history and the old attachments of land and family.

The Old Right worldview is constantly backward looking. It would agree with Allen Tate that the past should be in the present, or also with Weaver, who flatly declared that the past is the only thing that is real, and finally, with the equally blunt Faulkner, who famously praised his beloved Mississippi as a place where "the past isn't dead, it isn't even past." Americans should stay close to home. Young people should grow up living in the same town as their parents and grandparents. All those small-town Americans who have left their burgs and villages for the big city should return home again to build up their hometowns.

Paleoconservatives do not so much defend the family as much as they insist on its full autonomy from the state. In both rhetoric and policy, conservatives and liberals alike profess undying concern for the family. Tax credits, subsidies for day care centers, ending marriage taxes, and most of all, an endless fidelity to education spending (a subject that is an obsession among the public as well), animates such concerns. This wasn't always the case. There was a time when politicians left "the children" out of their speeches, knowing that child rearing was the business of parents and no one else. The Old Right dislikes public schools for the same reasons libertarians give: their purpose is brainwashing courtesy of the state. Again, the Old Right critique is impressive. Public schools are the invention of New Englanders, the first Americans to reject Christianity *en masse*. Parents should not raise their children, only public schoolmarms must do the job—or so gnostic New Englanders believed. The goal of public schools was to stop the spread of Christianity in the United States. Decades later, their operations are controlled by far-off regimes both in Washington and equally arrogant state capitols. Such was the criticism made by Kirk and Weaver even in the relatively placid 1950s. The curriculum at public schools has dropped to sub-Third World levels, but private and even religious schools have made their own contributions to the dumbing down of America. In his 1997 best seller, *Nearer My God*, William F. Buckley, Jr. revisited the New England prep school circuit, schools that at one time educated the nation's political and financial elite. Such schools, including Millbrook Academy in Connecticut (Buckley's own alma mater), now embraced non-Western religions and cultures in their curriculum, while giving short shrift to Christian holidays. Others, such as the Groton School in Massachusetts, continued to require daily chapel attendance, but the downhill slide towards Third World-worship was infecting all levels of American education, not just fever swamps in Berkeley or Madison.[12]

Despite the libertarians' brilliant dismissal of public schools, there is lingering sympathy for such institutions among some paleocons. Bill Kauffman recalls the days when public schools reflected the values of those citizens who paid for them. Schools were smaller, the kids knew each other, and parents knew other parents, too. Teachers often visited the homes of each student. Before the era of consolidation, a rural county might have three or four high schools, not one big factory for all young people. A teacher bringing in alien ideas to such schools would not last long. High school football and basketball teams, 4-H clubs, Latin clubs, drama clubs. All are part of the fabric of small communities, activities that prepare youngsters for adulthood. A young man who plays high school football is not going to the NFL, but he learns such virtues as discipline and sacrifice that will carry him through life.[13]

If public schools were locally owned and operated, then they would be worth saving. But this is not the case. Turning back the clock would take a public that can say no to federal "money for education." Such Beltway conservatives as Diane Ravitch and Chester Finn call for "national" standards, ones that might ignore the rich histories of regional cultures. Legislators in states as conservative as New Hampshire cave in to "Goals 2000" funding—and a multicultural-infested curriculum. As late as the 1950s, however, an august collection of college presidents denounced any federal aid to colleges and universities as a pernicious plan that would compromise the integrity of higher education. For decades, conservatives have enjoyed lampooning the follies on America's college campuses. Every fall, without fail, *National Review* publishes its annual education issue, usually mocking American colleges as expensive freak shows. To its credit, *NR* also publishes its own guide to the universities, highlighting those whose required curriculum remains true to America's founding Western heritage.

For Paul Gottfried, however, conservatives themselves hold some blame for the decline of higher education. Starting in the 1960s and 1970s, conservative scholars began abandoning the university for political activity. The emphasis on politics caused conservatives to simply ignore academic life, where, as Gottfried claims, they could have stayed and had an impact in both shaping intellectual trends and nurturing generations of young minds. "Second generation postwar conservatives underestimate the importance of culture as a precondition for political success," Gottfried has stated, echoing Leopold Tyrmand. As late as the 1960s, establishing traditionalist beachheads on college campuses was possible as universities were not nearly as hostile to conservative scholars and ideas as they are in these soft totalitarian, politically correct times. But according to Gottfried, conservatives of that era, "preferred networking to being scholars and thinkers." Hence, those conservatives who joined the think tank society in Washington were not driven from academia, rather they left because "they enjoy being in Washington and are socially indistinguishable from the 'new class' they denounce."[14]

An ambitious college professor can both teach and engage in some political activity. However, the teacher who can influence not one, but several generations of scholars is utterly indispensable. Consider the importance of Donald Davidson at Vanderbilt in keeping the flame of Southern traditionalism alive in an age of upheaval. One of his disciples was the young M.E. Bradford, who in turn, earned his own dedicated band of admirers, many of whom now do battle in the academic trenches. The same is true of Murray Rothbard's many students. Great teachers like Davidson, Bradford, and Rothbard are more important than scholars issuing position papers, even worthy ones, at well-funded Washington, D.C. think tanks. The leftist critic, Todd Gitlin, once complained that during the 1980s, while conservatives were "capturing" the White House, liberals took over the English Departments. Considering their preference for a non-activist presidency, the Old Right might think the English Department, in the long run, as a greater prize.

As opposed to vouchers, school choice, magnet schools, and other mild reforms, the Old Right rallied around the unexpected homeschooling revival of the 1990s. Titles from the Conservative Book Club and the Independent Institute's Liberty Fund were aimed to help parents that either home schooled their children or were considering the radical idea. Radical, indeed. Homeschooling, as Allan Carlson has pointed out, goes directly to the roots of American civilization. It was the way nearly all Americans were once educated. Early Americans severely disliked the idea of a formal education. Public schools, if they existed at all, were only in attendance for two or three months out of the entire year. Such parents would also allow churches to teach their children. As Andrew Lytle once recalled, that's how things usually were in the Old Republic. Education was the domain of the parents and the church. In such a scenario, the only schools were church schools.[15]

In homeschooling, Carlson saw "real hope" that a true revolution was at hand. The number of young people educated at home rose from a pithy 15,000 in the mid-1970s to up to 1.5 million twenty years later, with growth estimated at 15 percent a year. However, this phenomenon is not a cure-all. Sympathetic observers worried that homeschoolers would become spoiled. Clearly, the Old Right, still nostalgic for the days when public schools were indeed locally owned and operated, has some mixed feelings on the subject. Will homeschooled boys, for instance, ever know the joy of participating in organized sports? Will homeschoolers ever march in high school bands or play on sports teams that proudly bear the names of their hometowns on their jerseys? Still, as Fleming acknowledges, "all of us, in one way or another, are home schooled." Education is a never-ending process. It doesn't stop with a formal degree. Such college dropouts as William Faulkner, Ernest Hemingway, and F. Scott Fitzgerald were better read in the classics than today's average Ph.D candidate. Mary Pride counters the critics by noting that the "real world beckons." Homeschooled kids not only receive the kind of classical education now extinct in public schools and most private ones, they also get involved in "hands-on learning projects that draw the entire family together." In addition, they are given the opportunity for work or volunteering that "meets the child's interests, as opposed to politically correct 'community service.'" Homeschoolers also have "the chance to get out in the real world, instead of sitting at a desk eight hours a day." And yes, they are part of the "outside world" of 4-H clubs, church groups, and the local YMCA. Even if parents, for financial reasons, must send their children to public schools, they still need to turn off the television set and read to their youngsters.[16]

Fleming also urged parents to forego existing institutions by "setting up their own libraries and filling them with the classics of Christendom." That would include their personal home libraries, but also new institutions. Some hardy folk were willing to take up Fleming's challenge. When the U.S. Supreme Court, in a typically gratuitous decision, destroyed the all-male status of Virginia Military Institute, intrepid VMI alumni responded by making plans for a Southern Military Institute, their own private, all-male Christian university. Homeschoolers carried on by building their own university, one appropriately enough named for Patrick Henry. These are baby steps, but such new institutions could serve as beacons of excellence—and examples of moral courage that might inspire others.[17]

The homeschooling revolution is fine, but more is needed for any program of restoration to succeed. Also necessary is a return to the permanent things, the phrase coined by T.S. Eliot and later borrowed and advanced by Russell Kirk with great eloquence all throughout the latter's distinguished career. Conservatives, in their scholarship and rhetoric, need not only to stress the classics, but also to cultivate the ancient verities. The ideal education, in Kirk's view, would stress higher imagination over sensate triumph, the fear of God rather than "the mastery over man and nature," quality over quantity, justice over power, order over egotism, honor over success, and finally, in the "Socratic and Christian" tradition, the acknowledgment that the unexamined life is not worth living.[18]

Granting a concession to Hillary Clinton, it *does* "take a village" to raise children. Schooling, formal or otherwise, is important, but so are the influences from the church, the politics of a community, and the culture swirling all around young people. Instead of turning off the television, perhaps Americans should discard such contraptions altogether. A letter to the editor in the *Southern Partisan* recalled a Sunday sermon where the preacher declared the day was coming when one can tell a good Christian from a bad Christian by whether they have a television set in their house or not.

It does take a village. But for the Old Right, that hardly means Mrs. Clinton's oppressive, ever-growing, dominating state where parents risk losing their children simply for spanking them. Rather, it means Andrew Lytle's republic of families, a people with iron in their blood strong enough to reject "Pharaoh's schools" and all other temptations offered by their would-be masters in Washington, Manhattan, and Hollywood.

8

The Survival Question

From time to time, on the pages of the *Wall Street Journal,* the *Weekly Standard, National Review,* and *Human Events*, there appears strong criticism of the Republican Party. But at the end of the day, the right will stay in the GOP camp. Ever since 1964, when Barry Goldwater wrested the presidential nomination away from Nelson Rockefeller, conservatives have remained convinced that the GOP is "their" party. The rank-and-file is on their side. The Old Right, on the other hand, long ago left the Republican Party. In 1992, Murray Rothbard enthusiastically supported Pat Buchanan's challenge to George Bush. Once that contest ended, Rothbard signed on for Ross Perot's third-party run. Rothbard soon abandoned Perot, later declaring the Texas billionaire to be a "nut." But that fall, most leading paleos voted for Perot. In 1996, Old Rightists once again backed Buchanan in the primaries, but all were critical of his decision to endorse Bob Dole and forego the third-party option. In the spring of 1996, Buchanan was very much a force in American politics. The time was ripe to strike out on his own. Indeed, when Howard Phillips launched the U.S. Taxpayer's Party, it was designed, in part, to serve as a safe haven for such a Buchanan candidacy. But Buchanan, holding faint hopes for glory in 2000, said no. However, by the fall of 1999, Buchanan finally realized the GOP was no longer his political home. To the dismay of many—but certainly not all—conservatives, he left the party of his youth and began the difficult process of trying to make the Reform Party a lasting presence in American politics. A dismal performance by Buchanan in the 2000 elections proved his Old Right critics right: The commentator had waited too long in leaving the GOP. Buchananism had come and gone without seemingly leaving a trace on the body politic.

The Beltway Right is also satisfied with both the state of the American nation and the wisdom of the public. After all, look at who Americans have elected in recent decades: Richard Nixon, Ronald Reagan (two landslides), and in 1994, a Republican Congress. Conservatives firmly believe that the American people, in the end, can be counted on to vote the right way. As such, they would come to mock the old, more sober worldview that held sway on the Old Right. Ronald Reagan was an optimist. Look at where that got him. True, conservatives would always like more Republicans in Congress, but otherwise they remained supremely confident about the future of America: the economy is in great shape, technology will liberate us to greater and greater heights of wealth and prosperity. American military might can bring the world to heel.

The Old Right's pessimism (or realism) was simply a stern reminder that man is not only a slave to sin, but that the story of history itself is the rise and fall of nations. The Founding Fathers, a collection of men well versed in world history, would have considered it a great achievement if this new American republic lasted 500 years. In the wake of the gaudy 1980s-style conservative optimism, the Old Right revisited the somber side of things. True conservatives, Paul Gottfried claimed, always combine "short term pessimism with long term optimism." Old Right pessimism comes with a hard edge. Mostly, it zeroes in on the phenomenon of American decadence. Again, the Fleming influence is evident. Before he took over as editor of *Chronicles*, decadence was not a major theme of any journal on the right. Out of both frustration at watching America's ignoble, dishonorable slide into barbarism, and the knowledge that Americans were supposed to be a self-governing people, paleoconservatives often ridicule the masses as a collection of wimps unable, among other things, to turn off the television set. On the pages of *Chronicles*, the adult American public is derided as an "electorate of sheep" behaving as "trained seals" in front of their globalist masters. There is, as John Lukacs has maintained, the bad habit of Americans eventually adjusting to whatever trends emerge from the East or West Coasts, the colleges and universities, the government in Washington, and the entertainment industry. This means not only the acceptance of an American Empire, but also a public that tolerates obscene television shows and motion pictures, blasphemous taxpayer-supported "art," and anti-Western classroom propaganda. Americans are often seen as a people easily intimidated, easily cowed, easily brainwashed, a people without a soul, certainly a people without much spunk.

More to the point, there may not even *be* an "American people" anymore, if the term "a people" means shared values, beliefs, a shared culture, language, literature, history, and heritage. America still existed as a legal entity, but as a cultural entity, it was fading fast.[1]

Much Old Right criticism recalls H.L. Mencken's broadside against the emerging twentieth-century masses, the heirs to a free republic willing to throw away their heritage of liberty in return for entitlement state handouts. Paleoconservative concerns also echo Richard Weaver's analysis of the "spoiled child psychology," the title of the best chapter in *Ideas Have Consequences*. Modern man, Weaver declared, had given up the strenuous life, the grand struggle where his soul is at stake. Instead, he had succumbed to the "social security state," resulting in the pampered citizen of megalopolis now unfit "for struggle of any kind." Weaver published *Ideas* in 1948, when opposition to the New Deal was alive and kicking. Conservatives viewed things from a more defiant perspective. The welfare/warfare state was to be defeated. However, by 1980, even Ronald Reagan would not venture into such alien territory. Both the New Deal and the Great Society stood triumphant, unchallenged by conservative Republicans professing intense dislike for big government.[2]

So, there is the problem. Not just a supine GOP, but the public itself. Seventy years of cradle-to-grave welfare spending is a long time. Like the cult of immigration, the entitlement state is an idol that few Americans question. Some living Americans have memories of cultural unity in their country; few of them, however, have ever lived in a true republic.

Plus, there was the matter of the American landscape. Scattered shots have been fired against the regime. But there was also, to say the least, great apathy. Chilton Williamson, Jr. recalled graffiti in a California bar: "Another day, another 5,000 aliens." This was hardly a call to action, and Williamson has unhappily admitted to the lack of activism by ordinary Americans on the immigration crisis. While studying research by political scientist Donald Warren, Paul Gottfried observed that when it comes time to vote, the public cares more about keeping Social Security and Medicare intact than abolishing affirmative action or reducing immigration. Perhaps it *is* the economy that only matters. Such is the dilemma faced by the Old Right. And maybe an epitaph for the nation. George Bush used to enjoy taking out his wallet, slapping it, and declaring that this—and not any social or cultural issue—is what Americans really cared about.[3]

The question of American decadence loomed large. Americans, if public opinion polls are to be believed, express grave concerns about education, but remain satisfied with the computer-laden institutions their own children attend. To most suburban parents, technology is more important than the curriculum. Congress, and politicians in general, continued to receive low marks, but the voting public, in numbers that might make Joe Stalin blush, reelect their own legislators without nary a complaint. (In 1998, the reelection rate was over 98 percent.)

On other issues, Americans were left to their own devices, as the political class blissfully ignored pressing national concerns. On immigration, the consequences were demographic in several ways. America is a big country. And starting in the 1980s, Americans, in large numbers, moved out of entire states racked by uncontrolled immigration, a "tolerant" people fleeing diversity. Californians fled to Nevada, Oregon, Washington, Colorado, Utah, and elsewhere out West. For every Central American immigrant that moved into South Florida, a native moved out of Dade County and other neighboring municipalities. Northeasterners packed up and traveled not only to the old perennial, Florida, but now to Virginia, the Carolinas, and Georgia. In the 1990s alone, over one million people left the New York City metropolitan area. Politicians from the Midwest, especially Senators Spencer Abraham of Michigan and Mike DeWine of Ohio (both Republicans), steadfastly refused to consider immigration restrictions. There was some irony in their position. The once-mighty states of the industrial Midwest continued to lose congressional seats to such high-immigrant states as California, Texas, and Florida. That hardly bothered these two militant immigrationists.

The Old Right struggled against demographics caused not only by immigration, but also by American rootlessness. In the eighthteenth and nineteenth centuries, Americans settled the frontier, but once they laid down stakes, they often stayed put. Real communities were born. Likewise, there was little talk of values from politicians. Certain values were agreed upon and needed no explanation. During the War Between the States, hundreds of thousands of American boys traveled more than twenty miles outside their own homes for the first time in their lives. The twentieth century, however, was characterized by one upheaval after another: Industrialism, urban growth, the automobile, high and the breakdown of public school systems. Mass migrations of peoples followed. Millions of Americans, often through no fault of their own, were no longer rooted to the land beneath their feet. A civilized people have at least one foot firmly planted in the past. But the old America could hardly be real to such a mobile people.

At century's end, up to 30 percent of Americans lived outside of their home states. With such a rootless population, one oblivious to the land and its history, where were the "mystic chords of memory" necessary to unite Americans? Daniel Patrick Moynihan once claimed that a nation's citizens must at least *believe* they are related to each other. (One could not look at Moynihan's own voting record and read such statements without snickering.)[4]

Paul Gottfried saw such social revolutions as perhaps a fatal blow to the budding populism of the 1990s. Can such a movement overcome "a century of managerial consolidation" and the "administrative-therapeutic regime that seeks to interfere with every aspect of [American] life?" Referring to demographic trends, Gottfried also speculates that "[with] a mobile population, national communications network, and an international economy, it may be hard to recreate the kind of regional solidarity needed to curb federal administrators and federal judges." And finally, there are those great numbers of Americans who care more about material concerns than the culture war being waged by the left against the remaining remnants of American civilization.[5]

Changing demographics also meant a new suburban majority in America, one that replaced the old rural and small town predominance. Like Weaver, Eliot and other traditionalists, the Old Right held little hope for the complacent middle classes, including the "soccer moms" now being wooed by politicians. Bill Kauffman had fun sailing into this soccer phenomenon as an alien form of globalism invading the land of the free—and the home of baseball, football, basketball, prize-fighting, and stock car racing. Even editors at *National Review* fretted over the rise of soccer as yet another threat to a distinct American identity.

A bias toward small-town culture has always been a hallmark of the Old Right. In Bryan's day, it was the rural folk against the propagandists from the big-city tabloids. Those battles were still relevant, but paleos wondered if they had any allies in these hastily built suburbs. A vital regionalism rarely included the always chaotic urban life; it also could not flourish in the suburbs. Life is too transient, men commute to cities (or other suburbs), leaving early in the morning, returning in darkness to their "bedroom communities." Suburbs often lack a town square, a Main Street, a Church Street, boundaries and characteristics that separate them from other entities. No matter the location, parents should return to the old ways of raising children; first, by saying no to soccer and rides at the local theme park. Instead, fathers should teach boys the manly things: how to fish, hunt, split wood, to become thoroughly self-sufficient.

While acknowledging American decadence, the Old Right tried to make end runs around the regime. The League of the South, a heritage organization founded in part by Fleming and Wilson, revived the old Irish tradition of Hedge Schools, an initiative which kept Gaelic culture alive during the dark night of English occupation. Both the LOS and the Rockford Institute held summer school sessions stressing, among other disciplines, the classics, the literature and politics of Great Britain, the American South and Midwest; subjects now generally ignored by American colleges and universities. Such schools recalled Russell Kirk's famous summer seminars at Piety Hill in Mecosta, Michigan and M. Stanton Evans's educational program for aspiring conservative journalists. These new institutions could not reach the masses, but they might, in time, create a new hierarchy, a network of scholars among the rising generation. Fed up with the ongoing attacks on Southern history, LOS leaders began calling for "cultural independence" at their rallies, while blasting a "corrupt...sterile...national culture" one "repugnant to the Southern people and to every people with authentic Christian sensibilities."[6]

Other populists, inspired by Sam Francis's writings, claimed a Middle America revolution was still doable. Forget, at least for now, the complete libertarian agenda. Such a platform would still frighten the middle class. Concentrate instead on the "survival question," issues like an America First foreign policy that keeps the country out of needless wars, trade protection when deemed necessary, immigration restrictions, opposition to quotas, and in general, that same anti-American culture war. Alert and educate the public to the dangers posed by reckless policies on such issues. For instance, Americans continued to believe that there were more illegal aliens entering the country each year than legal immigrants; when in fact, legal alien entries outnumbered illegal ones by a good three to one margin.

This approach is similar to what Kevin Phillips, prophet of the old Republican Party's "lock" on the White House, advised in the 1960s. Working- and middle-class voters in the Nixon era liked Social Security; they disliked, however, campus radicals, school busing, excessive welfare programs, and abortion-on-demand. Focusing on those grievances allowed the Republicans to recover from Goldwater's 1964 landslide defeat. However, unless the GOP wakes up, the only vehicle for an Old Right platform is a third party. Ideally, a vote-getting third party would influence both the elephant and the donkey in a most positive manner. That might be too much to ask for in this age of supreme arrogance by the world's lone superpower. For the Old Right, the revolution begins at home. With persistence, it travels neighborhood by neighborhood, community by community, parish by parish. Sooner or later, however, there would have to be some political victories.

Either way, the Old Right faces a long road ahead. Every day is Monday. Pessimism aside, the rejuvenated Old Right and its worldview provides enormous benefits to those Americans willing to listen. Paleoconservatism amounts to a thorough education in Western and American history: where America came from, what the nation was intended to become, what it has disintegrated into, and how Americans might find their way back. American "exceptionalism" does not mean abstractions like democratic capitalism, but simply republican living. A republic means self-reliant citizens, like those early Americans "too proud and too poor" to live under a monarchy. It also means citizens who are active participants in the lives of their community and nation. The Old Right hopes to stir up the defiance of those "insubordinate Americans" who nourish the tree of liberty with their occasional rebellions. Paleos know that only a minority of peoples (not a "silent" majority) ever makes a true revolution. The road back to a republic is a hard one. Still, it is an American heritage most worth saving.

Notes

Introduction

1. Bill Kauffman, *America First!: Its History, Culture, And Politics*. Amherst, NY: Prometheus Books, 1995, p. 201.
2. For an early history of the conservative wars, see Lew Rockwell, "Realignment on the Right?" *Conservative Review,* vol. 1, no. 3, pp. 18-22.

1. Reading America

1. M.E. Bradford, "On Being Conservative in a Post-Liberal Era." *Intercollegiate Review*, Spring 1986, p. 18.
2. Thomas Fleming, "America, From Republic to Ant Farm." *Chronicles*, October 1991, p. 17.
3. For an overview of Dickinson's political thought, see M.E. Bradford, "A Better Guide Than Reason: The Politics of John Dickinson." From *A Better Guide Than Reason: Federalists & Anti-Federalists*. New Brunswick, NJ: Transaction Publishers, 1994, pp. 79-97.
4. Ibid, "According to Their Genius: Politics and the Example of Patrick Henry," pp. 97-111.
5. Murray Rothbard, "Life in the Old Right," *Chronicles*, August 1994, p. 16. Lew Rockwell, "Down With the Presidency," *Chronicles*, October 1997, p. 28.
6. Herbert Storing, *What the Anti-Federalists Were For*. Chicago: University of Chicago Press, 1981, pp. 19-20. Some anti-Federalists also predicted the Supreme Court would become a vehicle of judicial tyranny, while leading Federalists dismissed such dire prophecies.
7. Ibid, pp. 22-23.
8. Samuel Francis, "Nationalism, Old and New," *Chronicles*, June, 1992, p. 18.
9. William Murchison, "From Greeks to Gringos: How Mexico Lost Texas," *Chronicles*, July 1997, pp. 27-29.
10. Patrick J. Buchanan, *A Republic, Not An Empire: Reclaiming America's Destiny*. Washington, DC: Regnery, Publishing, 1999, pp. 115-122. On the issue of tariffs and the War of 1812, see Thomas DiLorenzo, "Yankee Confederates: New England Secession Movements." In *Secession, State, and Liberty*, David Gordon, editor. New Brunswick, NJ: Transaction Publishers, 1998, p. 147. On tariffs and the war between the states, see Charles Adams, *When In The Course of Human Events: Arguing the Case for Southern Secession*. Lanham, MD: Rowan & Littlefield Publishers, Inc., 2000, pp. 88-91.

118   **Revolt from the Heartland**

11. M.E. Bradford, "The Lincoln Legacy: The Long View," *Modern Age*, Fall 1980, p. 363. For another critique of the Gettysburg Address, see Adams, *When In the Course of Human Events*, pp. 193-200.
12. Bradford, "The Lincoln Legacy," pp. 359-360.
13. Frank Meyer, *The Conservative Mainstream*. New Rochelle, NY: Arlington House, 1964, pp. 470-472. Joseph Sobran, "Lincoln Loses a Fan," *Southern Partisan*, First Quarter, 1996, p. 6.
14. Richard M. Weaver, "Abraham Lincoln and The Argument From Definition." From *The Ethics of Rhetoric*. Davis, CA: Hermagoras Press, 1985, pp. 85-115. Russell Kirk, *The Roots of American Order*. Washington, DC: Regnery/Gateway, 1991, pp. 450-457. Andrew Nelson Lytle, "A Hero and the Doctrinaries of Defeat." *Georgia Review*, Winter 1956, pp. 65-66.
15. The GOP's old protectionism recalled in Patrick J. Buchanan, *The Great Betrayal: How American Sovereignty and Social Justice are Being Sacrificed to the Gods of the Global Economy*. Boston: Little Brown, 1998, p. 232, 239-240.
16. Ibid, p. 311.
17. The diverse opposition to the Spanish-American War noted in Buchanan, *A Republic, Not An Empire*, pp. 160-161.
18. Ibid, p. 161 for Bryan's shortcomings. Thomas Fleming, "From Bryan to Buchanan," *Chronicles*, March 1996, p. 9.
19. Bill Kauffman, "Who Do We Shoot?" *Chronicles*, March 1996, p. 18.
20. For an account of the coalition that defeated America's entry into the League of Nations, see Bill Kauffman, "Alice of Malice: The Other Side of Rooseveltism." From *American First!*, pp. 103-117.
21. Justin Raimondo, "The Lion of Idaho," *Chronicles*, November 1998, p. 24.
22. Chilton Williamson, Jr., *The Immigration Mystique: America's False Conscience*. New York: Basic Books, 1996, p. 54.
23. Samuel Francis, "Into History's Dustbin," *Chronicles*, November 1998, pp. 34-35.

2. The First Old Right

1. Murray Rothbard, *America's Great Depression*. New York: Richardson & Synder, 1983, pp. 32-33.
2. Patrick J. Buchanan, "Letter to the Editor," *Wall Street Journal*, April 27, 1998, p. 23
3. Ibid, p. 23.
4. For stinging criticism of the NRA, see Justin Raimondo, *Reclaiming the American Right: The Lost Legacy of the Conservative Movement*. Burlingame: Center for Libertarian Studies, 1993, pp. 132-133.
5. Earl Black and Merle Black, *The Vital South: How Presidents Are Elected*. Cambridge, MA: Harvard University Press, 1992, p. 91.
6. For a brief economic critique of early New Deal spending programs, see John T. Flynn, "The Experiment 'Noble in Purpose.'" From *Forgotten Lessons: Selected Essays of John T. Flynn*, Gregory P. Pavlik, editor. Irvington-on-Hudson, NY: The Foundation for Economic Education, 1996, pp. 60-66.
7. For grudging acknowledgement of the left's uncanny ability to use government to shape culture, see R. Emmett Tyrell, *The Conservative Crack-Up*. New York: Simon and Schuster, 1992, pp. 204-208.
8. Rothbard, "Life in the Old Right," p. 17.

9. Twelve Southerners, *I'll Stand My Stand: The South and the Agrarian Tradition*. Baton Rouge: Louisiana State Press, 1977, p. xliii.
10. Donald Davidson, "Regionalism In The Arts." From *Regionalism and Nationalism in the United States: The Attack on Leviathan*. New Brunswick, NJ: Transaction Publishers, 1992, pp. 65-101.
11. Ibid, pp. 11-12.
12. Wayne Cole, *Roosevelt and the Isolationalists*. Omaha: University of Nebraska Press, 1983, p. 415.
13. Rothbard, "Life in the Old Right," p. 17.
14. General Marshall's sentiments recalled in Ruth Salres Benedict, "The Anti-War Warriors," *Chronicles*, December 1991, p. 23.
15. Ronald Radosh, *Prophets on the Right: Profiles of Conservative Criticism of American Globalism*. New York: Simon and Schuster, 1975, pp. 53, 57.
16. *Roosevelt and The Isolationalists*, pp. 554-555. More criticism of the New Deal by Flynn in *Forgotten Lessons*, pp. 54-60.
17. For attacks on the bombing of Dresden and the entire concept of "total war," see John Denson, editor, *The Costs of War: America's Pyrrhic Victories*. New Brunswick, NJ: Transaction Publishers, 1997, p. 48, 353-54. Similar criticism in Richard M. Weaver, *Visions of Order: The Cultural Crisis of Our Time*. Wilmington: Intercollegiate Studies Institute, 1995, pp. 92-113.
18. Joseph Sobran, "Saving General Marshall," *New American*, September 14, 1998, pp. 34-35.
19. One of the many critiques of the performance of FDR and Churchill in Teheran and Yalta in Henry Regnery, "Winston Churchill: A Question of Leadership." From *A Few Reasonable Words: Selected Writings*. Wilmington: Intercollegiate Studies Institute, 1996, pp. 210-231. Harry Elmer Barnes, "The End of the Old America." *Modern Age*, Spring 1958, pp. 139-151. For Barnes, World War II also marked the end of the time-honored policy of American neutrality, which he saw as another cause for lament.
20. Andrew Lytle, "They Took Their Stand: The Agrarian View After Fifty Years." *Modern Age*, Spring 1980, pp. 114-120. Andrew J. Angyal, *Wendell Berry*. New York: Twayne Publishers, 1995, pp. 29, 60-61.

3. Cold War Conservatism

1. Rothbard, "Life in the Old Right," p. 15.
2. Ibid, p. 17.
3. Kauffman, *America First!*, p. 249.
4. William R. Rusher, *The Rise of the Right*. New York: William A. Morrow, 1984, p. 81.
5. Richard Weaver, *Ideas Have Consequences*. Chicago: University of Chicago Press, 1948, p. 170.
6. For reactions to *The Conservative Mind* by the author himself, see Russell Kirk, *The Sword of Imagination: Memoirs of a Half Century of Literary Conflict*. Grand Rapids, MI: William B. Eerdmans Company, 1995, pp. 148-152.
7. Conservative in-fighting over Hungary in John Judis, *William F. Buckley, Jr.: Patron Saint of the Conservatives*. New York: Simon and Schuster, 1988, pp. 150-153.
8. Hull's ideas on trade in *The Great Betrayal: How American Sovereignty and Social Justice Are* , pp. 21-24, 58.

120   Revolt from the Heartland

9. Ibid, p. 25-38.
10. William F. Buckley, *Nearer My God*, Boston: Little, Brown, 1999, pp. 91-108 and Patrick J. Buchanan, *Right From The Beginning*, Boston: Little,Brown, 1988, pp. 78-79 for devastating analysis of the consequences of Vatican II.
11. Weaver, *Visions of Order*, p. 21.
12. Buckley's support for a domestic big government recalled in Paul Gottfried, "Conservative Crack-Up Continued," *Society*, January/February 1994, p. 26.
13. Burnham's Cold War strategy analyzed in George Nash, *The Conservative Intellectual Movement in America: Since 1945*. Wilmington, DE: Intercollegiate Studies Institute, 1996, pp. 81-87.
14. Ibid, pp. 11-112.
15. Rusher, *The Rise of the Right*, p. 163.
16. Judis, *William F. Buckley: Patron Saint of the Conservatives*, p. 402.
17. Paul Gottfried, "A View of Contemporary Conservatism," *The Intercollegiate Review*, Spring 1986, p. 19. *The Conservative Movement*, p. 115.
18. Irving Kristol, *Neoconservatism: The Autobiography of an Idea*. New York: The Free Press, 1995, p. 29.
19. Ibid, p. xi, 379.
20. Paul Gottfried, *The Conservative Movement* (revised edition). New York: Twayne Publishers, 1993, pp. 84-85.

4. The Chapel Hill Conspiracy

1. William F. Buckley, Jr., "An Agenda for the Nineties," *National Review*, February 19, 1990, pp. 34-40.
2. Gottfried, *The Conservative Movement* (revised edition), p. 144.
3. Episode recounted in an obituary/tribute to Percy by Thomas Fleming in the September 1990 *Chronicles*, p. 9.
4. Samuel Francis, "Foreign Policy and the South," pp. 91-105; M.E. Bradford, "Not in Memoriam, But in Affirmation," pp. 212-224; Andrew Lytle, "Afterword: A Semi-Centennial, pp. 224-231. All from Fifteen Southerners, *Why the South Will Survive*, Clyde Wilson, editor. Athens: University of Georgia Press, 1981.
5. Samuel Francis, "Message from MARS: The Social Politics of the New Right," pp. 64-84; Clyde Wilson, "Citizens or Subjects?" pp. 106-128; Thomas Fleming, "Old Rights and The New Right," pp. 180-205. All from *The New Right Papers*, Robert Whittaker, editor. New York: St. Martin's Press, 1982.
6. "A Special Message to Our Readers Old and New...," *Southern Partisan*, Spring/Summer, 1981, p. 1.
7. Richard Quinn, "Partisan View," *Southern Partisan*, Spring, 1982, p. 4.
8. "Report From the Capitols," *Southern Partisan,* Fall, 1981, pp. 4-5.
9. Years later, Joseph Sobran would charge that his former allies on the right had simply abandoned the U.S. Constitution. All conservatives had to keep saying was that such spending programs were patently unconstitutional. In the Constitution, conservatives had a great weapon to fight leviathan. Smitten by the idea of an America empire creating a global democracy, they failed to use it.
10. Thomas Fleming, Paul Gottfried. *The Conservative Movement*. New York; Twayne Publishers, 1988, p. 43.
11. Thomas Fleming, "The Emperor's Tattoo," *Chronicles,* May 2000, p. 10.
12. Samuel Francis, *Beautiful Losers: Essays on the Failure of American Conservatism*. Columbia: University of Missouri Press, 1993, p. 159. See Thomas Fleming, "Vandals in the Academy" *Chronicles,* September 1990, p. 13 where Fleming

claimed the assault on the classics was "more important perhaps than the collapse of communism in Eastern Europe." What good was it to win the Cold War, when at home, the nation was losing its Western heritage? Wasn't that heritage the reason the Cold War was fought in the first place?

13. M.E. Bradford, "Rhetoric and Responsibility: Conservatives and the Problem of Language," *Modern Age,* Summer 1989, pp. 238-243.

14. Fleming has said he left *Southern Partisan* after the new publishers did not keep a written promise guranteeing him editorial autonomy.

5. Suicide of the West—Again

1. Thomas Fleming, "A Not So Wonderful Life," *Chronicles,* July 1990, p. 12. The title of this chapter refers to James Burnham's 1964 book, *Suicide of the West: An Essay on the Meaning and Destiny of Liberalism.* Washington: Regnery-Gateway, 1989. For Burnham the "suicide" was caused not only by decolonization and retreat in the face of comunism, but by a liberalism that did not believe in the survival of Western civilization itself anywhere in the world.

2. Scott McConnell, "Elegy for a Contrarian," *National Interest,* Summer 1998, pp. 81-83.

3. Ibid, p. 84.

4. See Patrick J. Buchanan, *The Death of the West: How Dying Populations and Immigrant Invasions Imperil Our Country and Civilization.* Thomas Dunne Books: New York, 2002, pp. 25-51 for grim statistics on the birth death crisis.

5. The irony is that Al Smith, in trying to appeal to Middle America and to downplay the idea that his Catholicism represented a threat to the old America, campaigned in favor of immigration restrictions during his unsuccessful 1928 run for the White House.

6. Williamson, *The Immigration Mystique,* pp. 64-65.

7. Ibid, pp. 67-69.

8. Ibid, p. 117. Peter Brimelow, *Alien Nation: Common Sense on America's Immigration Disaster.* New York: Random House, 1995, pp. 251-253 for the zero immigration policies of Asian and Central American nations.

9. Williamson, *The Immigration Mystique,* pp. 70-71.

10. Brimelow, *Alien Nation,* p. 84.

11. Clyde Wilson, "As a City Upon a Hill," *Chronicles,* June 1985, p. 20.

12. Mark Gerson, *The Neoconservative Vision: from the Cold War to the Culture Wars.* Lanham, MD: Madison Books, 1996, p. 310.

13. Donald Huddle, "The Cost of Immigration," *Chronicles,* March 1994, p. 20.

14. M.E. Bradford, "Sentiment or Survival: The Case Against Amnesty." *American Spectator,* April 1984, pp. 19-22.

15. For examples, see M.E. Bradford, "A Teaching for Republicans: Roman History and the Nation's First Identity." *A Better Guide Than Reason: Federalists and anti-Federalists.* New Brunswick, NJ: Transaction Publishers, 1994, pp. 3-27. See the Summer 1999 number of *The University Bookman* for essays that also revisit the classical influence on the Founding Fathers.

16. Concerning the Southwest itself, immigration threatened to be a vehicle used to settle some old scores. Starting in the 1970s, grumblings could be heard in the Southwest of an "Aztlan" in the making. Once Mexican immigrants and their offspring commanded solid majorities in California, Texas, and other states, they would vote themselves out of the union, creating a new nation or perhaps, reuniting such states with Mexico. Even if street gang members were the only ones

making such noises, it would be a cause for concern. Eventually, even those in higher positions voiced revolutionary rhetoric. In 1996, Mexican President Ernesto Zedillo traveled to Dallas to tell a Mexican-American audience that they were Mexicans who just happened to be living in the United States. Others began beating the drums for nationhood. "We will one day be a majority and reclaim our birthright by any means necessary—and we shouldn't shy away [from it]," declared one Charles Truxillo, a professor of Chicano studies at the University of New Mexico. Similar inflammatory language is cited in Roger D. McGrath, "The Reconquista of California," *Chronicles*, October 2000, pp. 34-38.

17. The moral argument has been made most forcibly by Williamson and Brimelow.
18. Gottfried, *The Conservative Movement* (revised edition), p. 137 for reports of Feulner's threats.
19. Paul Colford, *The Rush Limbaugh Story: Talent on Loan from God*. New York: St. Martin's Press, 1993, pp. 164-166.
20. The phrase belongs to Chilton Williamson, Jr. made in *The Immigration Mystique*, p. 99.

6. Against American Empire

1. Thomas Fleming, "Remembering the Maine," *Chronicles*, August 1999, p. 12.
2. Lew Rockwell, "The Case for Paleo-libertarians," *Liberty,* November 1990, pp. 34-38.
3. Raimondo, *Reclaiming the American Right*, p. 214, 217.
4. M.E. Bradford, "Is the American Experience Conservative?" In *The Reactionary Imperative: Essays Literary and Political*. Peru, IL: Sherwood Sugden and Company, 1990, p. 138.
5. Fleming quoted in David Frum, *Dead Right*. New York: New Republic Books, 1994, p. 156.
6. Thomas Fleming, "The Only Game in Town," *Chronicles*, June 1999, p. 12. Srdja Trifkovic, "Defending the West...Against Itself," *Chronicles*, August 1999, p. 24.
7. Samuel Francis, "The Price of Empire," *Chronicles*, June 1997, pp. 14-18. On Cato's problems, see *The Conservative Movement* (revised edition), pp. 135-136.
8. The weekly death count from Iraq cited in Justin Raimondo, "No Peace for Iraq," *Chronicles*, March 2000, pp. 44-45.
9. On America's brushes with catastrophe on the terrorist front, see Patrick J. Buchanan, "Cataclysmic Terror Ahead?" *Southern Partisan*, Fourth Quarter, 1998, p. 51.
10. For an Old Right appreciation of Senator Fulbright, see Bill Kauffman, "Fulbright: The First Arkansas Bill." From *America First!*, pp. 143-155.

7. What the Old Right is For

1. Allan Carlson, "The Military as an Engine of Social Change," pp. 389-399; Samuel Francis, "Classical Republicans and the Right to Bear Arms," pp. 53-67; Murray Rothbard, "America's Two Just Wars: 1775 and 1861," pp. 119-135, all from *The Costs of War*.
2. Hans-Herman Hoppe, "The Economic and Political Rationale for European Secessionism," pp. 191-225; Murray Rothbard, "Nations By Consent: Decompos-

ing the Nation-State," pp. 79-89; Clyde Wilson, "Secession: The Last, Best Bulwark of Our Liberties," pp. 89-99, all from *Secession, State & Liberty*.

3. The Von Mises flyer for "A Conference on Presidential Tyranny" was published in, among other places, the *Southern Partisan*, Second Quarter, 1998.

4. James Burnham, *Congress and The American Tradition*. Chicago: Henry Regnery Company, 1959. Even though Newt Gingrich, while Speaker of the House, went along with President Bill Clinton's globalist agenda, he still has publicly recommended this book.

5. Peter Grier, "New Political Tags: Global vs. National," *Christian Science Monitor*, December 22, 1997. p. 1, 14.

6. For chapters on interstate highways and military life as especially representing threats to family life and the social fabric of once-cohesive, contended communities, see Bill Kauffman, *With Good Intentions? Reflections on the Myth of Progress in America*. Westport: Praeger Books, 1997, pp. 1-33, 83-117.

7. Chilton Williamson, Jr. "The Frontier: America's Broken Template." *Chronicles*, August 1995, pp. 18-22.

8. Allan Carlson, "The Midwestern Identity," *Chronicles*, August 1995, pp. 22-25.

9. Michael Hill, "The South and The New Reconstruction," *Chronicles*, March 1992, pp. 21-24.

10. Bill Kauffman, "New York vs. New York," *Chronicles*, January 1991, p. 20.

11. Ibid, p. 21.

12. Buckley, *Nearer My God*, pp. 290-300.

13. For a lament on the demise of rural school district in America, see Bill Kauffman, "Weatherbeaten Shacks, Ignorant Parents: What's Behind School Consolidation?" In *With Good Intentions?*, pp. 33-49. In 1937, for instance, the United States counted 127,531 school districts. By 1992, that number had dropped to 14,556.

14. Paul Gottfried, "Letter to the Editor," *Southern Partisan*, Second Quarter, 1996, p. 2. Similar analysis made by Gottfried in *The Conservative Movement* (revised edition), pp. 71-72.

15. For an overview on the homeschooling phenomenon, see Allan Carlson, "From Cottage to Work Station...And Back Again: The Family and Home Education." *The Family in America*, February 1996, pp. 1-8. Testimony to the ways of the Old Republic given by Andrew Lytle in "Partisan Conversation," *Southern Partisan*, Second Quarter, 1991, pp. 27-37.

16. Mary Pride, "Star Trek or Star Wars?: Two Futures for American Education." *Chronicles*, September 1999, p. 15.

17. Thomas Fleming puts down the challenge in "Trollopes in the Stacks." *Chronicles*, April 1993, pp. 12-15.

18. Russell Kirk, *Academic Freedom: An Essay in Definition*. Chicago: Henry Regnery and Company, 1955, pp. 190-191.

8. The Survival Question

1. The habit of Americans "eventually accepting anything," is a major theme in John Lukacs, *The Thread of Years*. New Haven, CT: Yale University Press, 1999.

2. Weaver, *Ideas Have Consequences*, pp. 113-129.

3. Williamson, *The Immigration Mystique*, p. 5.

4. Kauffman, *With Good Intentions?*, p. 95.

5. Paul Gottfried, "Whither the Populist Wave?" *Chronicles*, July 1996, pp. 22-24.

6. From a "Declaration of Southern Cultural Independence," *Southern Patriot*, March-April 2000, p. 4.

Bibliography

Books from the past decade that are primers to current Old Right thinking are: M.E. Bradford, *Against the Barbarians and Other Reflections on Familiar Themes* (Columbia: University of Missouri Press, 1992); Russell Kirk, *America's British Culture* (New Brunswick, NJ: Transaction Publishers, 1993); Samuel Francis, *Beautiful Losers: Essays on the Failure of American Conservatism* (Columbia: University of Missouri Press, 1993); Paul Gottfried, *The Conservative Movement* (revised edition) (New York: Twayne Publishers, 1993); Justin Raimondo, *Reclaiming the American Right: The Lost Legacy of the Conservative Movement* (Burlingame: Center for Libertarian Studies, 1993); Bill Kauffman, *America First! Its History, Culture, and Politics* (Amherst, NY: Prometheus Press, 1995); Thomas Fleming, (editor) *Immigration and the American Identity: Selections from Chronicles: A Magazine of American Culture, 1985-1995*, (Rockford, IL: The Rockford Institute, 1995); Chilton Williamson, Jr., *The Immigration Mystique: America's False Conscience* (New York: Basic Books, 1996); Joseph Scotchie, (editor) *The Paleoconservatives: New Voices of The Old Right* (New Brunswick, NJ: Transaction Publishers, 1999); John Denson, (editor) *The Costs of War: America's Phyrric Victories*, (New Brunswick, NJ: Transaction Publishers, 1997); David Gordon, (editor) *Secession, State and Liberty* (New Brunswick, NJ: Transaction Publishers, 1998); Patrick J. Buchanan, *A Republic, Not An Empire: Reclaiming America's Destiny* (Washington, DC: Regnery Gateway, 1999).

Agar, Herbert, Tate, Allen (editors). *Who Owns America? A New Declaration of Independence*. Wilmington, DE: Intercollegiate Studies Institute Press, 1999.

Barnes, Harry Elmer. *Revisionism: A Key to Peace and Other Essays*. San Francisco, CA: Cato Institute, 1980.

Beard, Charles A. *American Foreign Policy in the Making, 1932-1940*. New Haven, CT: Yale University Press, 1946.

Bradford, M.E. *A Better Guide Than Reason: Federalist and Anti-Federalists*. LaSalle, IL: Sherwood Sugden, 1979. Reissued by Transaction Publishers, New Brunswick, NJ, 1994.

—.*A Worthy Company: Brief Lives of the Framers of the Constitution.* Marlborough, NH: Plymouth Rock Foundation, 1982.

—.*Generations of the Faithful Heart: On the Literature of the South.* LaSalle, IL: Sherwood Sugden, 1983.

—.*Remembering Who We Are: Reflections of a Southern Conservative.* Athens: The University of Georgia Press, 1985.

—.*The Reactionary Imperative: Essays Literary and Political.* Peru, IL: Sherwood Sugden, 1990.

—.*Original Intentions: On the Making and Ratification of the United States Constitutions.* Athens: The University of Georgia Press, 1993.

Brimelow, Peter. *Alien Nation: Common Sense About America's Immigration Disaster.* New York: Random House, 1995.

Buchanan, Patrick J. *Conservative Votes, Liberal Victories: Why the Right Has Failed.* New York: Quadrangle/New York Times Book Company, 1975.

—.*The Great Betrayal: How American Sovereignty and Social Justice Are Being Sacrificed to the Gods of the Global Economy.* Boston: Little, Brown, 1998.

Burnham, James. *The Managerial Revolution.* Bloomington: Indiana University Press, 1940.

—.*The Machiavellians: Defenders of Freedom.* Chicago: Henry Regnery Company, 1943.

—.*The Struggle for the World.* New York: The John Day Company, 1947.

—.*The Coming Defeat of Communism.* New York: The John Day Company, 1950.

—.*Containment or Liberation? An Inquiry into the Aims of U.S. Foreign Policy.* New York: The John Day Company, 1953.

—.*Congress and the American Tradition.* Chicago: Henry Regnery Company, 1959.

—.*Suicide of the West: An Essay on the Meaning and Destiny of Liberalism.* New York: The John Day Company, 1964.

Carlson, Allan. *The Swedish Experiment in Family Politics: The Myrdals and the Interwar Population Crisis.* New Brunswick, NJ: Transaction Publishers, 1990.

—.*The Family: Is it Just Another Lifestyle Choice?* London: FA Health and Welfare Unit, 1993.

—.*From Cottage to Work Station: The Family's Search for Social Harmony in the Industrial Age.* San Francisco, CA: Ignatius Press, 1993.

Chodorov, Frank. *The Rise and Fall of Society: An Essay on the Economic Forces that Underlie Social Institutions.* New York: Devin-Adair, 1959.

—.*Out of Step: The Autobiography of An Individualist.* New York: Devin-Adair, 1962.

Cole, Wayne S. *Roosevelt and the Isolationists.* Omaha: University of Nebraska Press, 1983.

Davidson, Donald. *The Attack on Leviathan: Regionalism and Nationalism in the United States*. Chapel Hill: University of North Carolina Press, 1938. Reissued by Transaction Publishers, New Brunswick, N.J., 1990.

——.*Still Rebels, Still Yankees*. Baton Rouge: Louisiana State University Press, 1957. Reissued by the same publisher in 1972.

Fleming, Thomas. *The Politics of Human Nature*. New Brunswick, NJ: Transaction Publishers, 1988.

——.(with Paul Gottfried), *The Conservative Movement*. Boston: Twayne Publishers, 1988.

Flynn, John T. *The Roosevelt Myth*. New York: Devin-Adair, 1948.

——.*The Decline of the American Republic and How to Rebuild It*. New York: Devin-Adair, 1955.

——.*As We Go Marching*. New York: Arno Press, 1972.

——.*Forgotten Lessons: Selected Essays of John T. Flynn* (edited by Gregory P. Pavlik). Irvington-on-Hudson, NY: The Foundation for Economic Education, Inc., 1996.

Francis, Samuel. *Power and History: The Political Thought of James Burnham*. Lanham, MD: University Press of America, 1984.

——.*Revolution from the Middle: Columns and Articles from Chronicles, 1989-1996*. Raleigh, NC: Middle American Press, 1997.

Garret, Garet. *The American Story*. Chicago: Henry Regnery Co., 1955.

Gottfried, Paul. *Conservative Millenarians: The Romantic Experience in Bavaria*. New York: Fordham University Press, 1979.

——.*The Search for Historical Meaning: Hegel and the Postwar American Right*. DeKalb, IL: Northern University Press, 1986.

——.(with Thomas Fleming) *The Conservative Movement*. Boston: Twayne Publishers, 1988.

——.*Carl Schmitt: Politics and Theory*. New York: Greenwood Press, 1990.

——.*After Liberalism: Mass Democracy and the Managerial State*. New Haven, CT: Yale University Press, 1999.

Hummel, Jeffrey. *Emancipating Slaves, Enslaving Free Men*. Peru, IL: Open Court Press, 1996.

Kauffman, Bill. *Every Man A King*. New York: Soho Press, 1989.

——.*With Good Intentions: Reflections on the Myth of Progress in America*. Westport, CT: Praeger, 1998.

Kirk, Russell. *Randolph of Roanoke: A Study in Conservative Thought*. Chicago: University of Chicago Press, 1951.

——.*The Conservative Mind: From Burke to Santayana*. Chicago: Henry Regnery Company, 1953. (This book has gone through seven editions, the latest titled *The Conservative Mind: From Burke to Eliot*, published also by Regnery in 1994.)

——.*Beyond the Dreams of Avarice: Essays of a Social Critic*. Chicago: Henry Regnery Company, 1956.

—.*A Program for Conservatives*. Chicago: Henry Regnery Company, 1962.

—.*Confessions of a Bohemian Tory: Episodes and Reflections of a Vagrant Career*. New York: Fleet Publishing Corp., 1963.

—.(with James McClellan), *The Political Principles of Robert A. Taft*. New York: Fleet Publishing Corp., 1967.

—.*Enemies of the Permanent Things: Observations of Abnormality in Literature and Politics*. New Rochelle, NY: Arlington House, 1969.

—.*Eliot and His Age: T.S. Eliot's Moral Imagination in the Twentieth Century*. New York: Random House, 1971.

—.*The Roots of American Order*. LaSalle, IL: Open Court, 1974.

—.*Decadence and Renewal in the Higher Learning: An Episodic History of American University and College Since 1953*. South Bend, IN: Gateway Editions, 1978.

—.*Edmund Burke: A Genius Reconsidered*. Peru, IL: Sherwood Sugden, 1988.

—.*The Conservative Constitution*. Washington, DC: Regnery Gateway, 1990.

—.*The Politics of Prudence*. Bryn Mawr, PA: Intercollegiate Studies Institute, 1993.

—.*Redeeming the Time*. Wilmington, DE: Intercollegiate Studies Institute, 1997.

Lane, Rose Wilder. *The Discovery of Freedom: Man's Struggle Against Authority*. New York: John Day, 1943.

Lytle, Andrew. *From Eden to Babylon: The Social and Political Essays of Andrew Nelson Lytle* (edited by M.E. Bradford). Washington, DC: Regnery Gateway, 1990.

Meyer, Frank S. *What Is Conservatism?* New York: Holt, Rinehart and Winston, 1964.

—.*In Defense of Freedom and Related Essays*. Indianapolis, IN: Liberty Fund, 1996.

Nock, Albert Jay. *Our Enemy, The State*. Caldwell, ID: Caxton, 1946.

Paterson, Isabel. *The God of the Machine*. New York: Putnam, 1943.

Radosh, Ronald. *Prophets on The Right: Conservative Critics of American Globalism*. New York: Simon & Schuster, 1975.

Rockwell, Llewellyn, H. *The Gold Standard: An Austrian Perspective* (editor). Lexington, MA: Lexington Books, 1985.

—.*The Case for Paleolibertarianism and Realignment on the Right*. Burlingame: Center for Libertarian Studies, 1990.

Rothbard, Murray. *Man, Economy and State: A Treatise on Economic Principles*. Princeton, NJ: Van Nostrand, 1962.

—.*America's Great Depression*. Los Angeles: Nash Publishers, 1972.

—.*For A New Liberty*. New York: Macmillan, 1973.

—.*Conceived in Liberty*, three volumes. New Rochelle, NY: Arlington House, 1975-1979.

—.*Individualism and the Philosophy of Social Sciences*. San Francisco, CA: The Cato Institute, 1979.

—.*The Case Against the Fed*. Auburn, AL: Ludwig von Mises Institute, 1994.

Storing, Herbert J. *What the Anti-Federalists Were For*. Chicago: University of Chicago Press, 1891.

Taft, Robert A. *A Foreign Policy for Americans*. Garden City, NY: Doubleday, 1951.

Twelve Southerners. *I'll Take My Stand: The South and the Agrarian Tradition*. Baton Rouge: Louisiana State University Press, 1977.

Weaver, Richard. *Ideas Have Consequences*. Chicago: The University of Chicago Press, 1948.

—.*The Ethics of Rhetoric*. Chicago: Henry Regnery Company, 1953. Reissued by Hermagoras Press, Davis, CA: 1985.

—.*Visions of Order: The Cultural Crisis of Our Time*. Baton Rouge: Louisiana State University Press, 1964. Reissued by Intercollegiate Studies Institute, 1995.

—.*Life Without Prejudice and Other Essays*. Chicago: Henry Regnery Company, 1965.

—.*The Southern Tradition at Bay: A Study of Postbellum Literature* (edited by M.E. Bradford and George Core). New Rochelle, NY: Arlington House, 1968. Reissued by Regnery/Gateway, Washington, DC, 1989.

—.*The Southern Essays of Richard M. Weaver* (edited by George M. Curtis III and James J. Thompson). Indianapolis, IN: Liberty Press, 1987.

—.*In Defense of Tradition* (edited by Ted J. Smith). Indianapolis, IN: Liberty Fund, 2000.

Wilson, Clyde. *Why the South Will Survive: Fifteen Southerners Look at Their Region a Half Century After I'll Take My Stand* (editor). Athens: University of Georgia Press, 1980.

—.*The Essential Calhoun: Selections from Writings, Speeches, and Letters* (editor). New Brunswick, NJ: Transaction Publishers, 1992.

Index

Himmlefarb, Gertrude, 60
Hines, Richard, 55
Hitler, Adolf, 22-23, 26, 96
Hook, Sidney, 44
Hoover, Herbert, 15-16, 23
Hopkins, Harry, 18
Hoppe, Hans-Herman, 95
Howard, John, 61
Hull, Cordell, 35
Human Events, 95, 101, 109
Hume, David, 42
Humphrey, Hubert, 57
Hussein, Saddam, 82-83
Hutchinson, Kay Bailey, 73

Ideas Have Consequences (Weaver), 32, 111
I'll Take My Stand (Twelve Southern-ers), 19-20
Immigration Mystique, The (Williamson), 63
Independent Institute, 106
International Monetary Fund, 90
Ionesco, Eugene, 66

Jack Paar Show, The, 32
Jackson, Henry, 61,
Jackson, Robert H., 18
Jefferson, Thomas, 5, 33, 55, 59, 90, 97
Johnson, Hugh, 16
Johnson, Lyndon, B., 35, 39-40, 61, 67, 96
Joyce, James, 21

Kauffman, Bill, vii-viii, 26, 39, 50, 102
Kazin, Alfred, 102
Kemp, Jack, 61, 75
Kendall, Willmoore, 11, 32-3, 43
Kennedy, Edward, 68
Kennedy, John F., 35, 38, 61, 67
Kennedy, William, 102
Kerouac, Jack, 61
Khruschev, Nikita, 38
Kilpatrick, James J., 36, 40
King George III, 3
King Jr., Martin Luther, 59, 61
Kirk, Russell, 1-2, 8, 25, 30, 32, 33, 35, 37, 38, 43, 54, 55, 81, 103, 104
Kirkpatrick, Jeane, 81
Kristol, Irving, 44-45, 49, 57
Kristol, William, 61, 101

Lane, Rose Wilder, 19
Landess, Thomas, 2
Lanier, Lyle, 52
Lawrence, D.H., 21
League of Nations, 12
League of the South, 114
Let Your Mind Alone (Thurber), 30
Lee, Robert E., 59
Lewis, Sinclair, 103
Limbaugh, Rush, 58, 75, 98
Lincoln, Abraham, 5-9, 16, 57, 96
Lindsay, John, 40
Lindsay, Vachel, 20
Lodge, Henry Cabot, 12
Longworth, Alice Roosevelt, 12
Lowry, Rich, 76
Lukacs, John, 110
Ludwig Von Mises Institute, 79, 93, 94-97
Lytle, Andrew, 8, 14, 19, 27, 52, 53, 103, 106, 108

MacLeish, Archibald, 18
Macmillan, Harold, 34
Madison, James, 2, 100
Mailer, Norman, 103
Managerial Revolution, The, 21
Marshall, George, 23, 25
Mason, George, 80
Masters, Edgar Lee, 7, 14, 20
McCarthy, Joseph, 44
McConnell, Scott, 76, 85
McCormick, Robert, 13, 16
McDonald, Forrest, 103
McKinley, William, 9-10
McLaughlin, John, 64
Meese, Edwin, 60
Meet the Press, 32
Mencken, H.L., 7, 13, 19, 24
"Message from MARs," (Francis), 53
Meyer, Frank, 7, 32-33, 35
Midland, The, 20
Milosevic, Slobodan, 83-84, 97
Mondale, Walter, 46
Montgomery, Marion, 52
Moynihan, Daniel, 20

NAFTA, 93, 94, 98
Nader, Ralph, vii, 98
Nasser, Gamal, 34
National Interest, The, 76